Banx

A dog from scratch, literally

Darragh O'Gowner

ZIZICOCOART PUBLISHING

First published in Great Britain in 2020

ISBN 0-9542289-2-8

For Dordor

PAWWORD

This is not a book about how to train your dog, far from it, it's perhaps more like how not to train it. Nor is it about a heroic dog, who went into a burning building and rescued people, nor one that sniffed out billions of tons of cocaine at some airport. Neither is it about a dog so smart that it has a double first in History from Cambridge. No. Definitely not. This is about one dog's journey in this world and his impact on us. It's not "sugar-coated-lovey-dovey" stuff, this is a brutally honest account of the highs and lows of owning a dog, from scratch, literally.......

JINGLE BELLS

Like a tattoo, a dog is for life, not just for Christmas. With both of us still working in full-time jobs it might be a little awkward, dog sitting, but I was sure it could be done, couldn't it? After all it can't be that difficult, can it?

There had been much furtive stuff going on in the lead up to Christmas. Yes it had to be 'the big secret' coming to life – at last. What a Christmas to remember......

PART 1

ARE YOU EXPERIENCED?

Dogs were the first animals to be domesticated by nomadic hunters, around 15,000 years ago, and today are the most widely abundant land based carnivore. Over this time they have become very adapted to human behaviour and while predominantly they act as pets, they are also used in roles such as guide-dogs, hearing-dogs, sheep-dogs, guard-dogs and as therapy for people suffering with mental health issues. Because of this, they have acquired the label of "Man's best friend".

I wonder what dogs themselves think of Man? I wonder what dogs think full stop? If only they could tell us. Curious creatures, mainly lovable – why haven't I got one?

I don't remember having a particular craving to have one as a pet in my childhood, it was one of those things that never came up in conversation at home. If it did it would have been quickly dismissed. And up until we became parents ourselves, I don't think it was ever discussed seriously. If anything it was something we definitely didn't want, having witnessed what some dog owners went through – the image of my brother-in-law cooking Sunday roast and picking up a turd from the kitchen floor, that had been dumped there by their dog, without a worry about hygiene, was enough to put anyone off – wasn't it?

But I couldn't deny that I had some very happy reminiscences of dogs......my first encounter, that I can properly recall, would have been when I was about 5 or 6. My uncle had a dog called "Kimmy" possibly the love child of a Corgi and a Labrador but very firmly a "Heinz 57" mongrel. I have fond memories of my uncle throwing a ball in a hedge and the dog actually getting right on top of it and then drilling its way inside, working its way along to retrieve the ball. Most amusing. Kimmy and my uncle had a symbiotic relationship in that they both idolised each other. Unbeknown to me at the time, and something I only learned of much later in life, he suffered badly from depression. I suspect that Kimmy was his 'treatment' which was a far better solution than the ECT often on offer, my mother was a regular for that.

Then there was "Muffin" my grandfather's dog, whose party trick was to eat sweets from his mouth, "Penny" a truly fat Corgi that my aunt owned, who didn't do much other than act as a model for my fat cousin, "Lucky" the black arrow of a dog that I don't remember much about other than it elicited the phrase (from the same aunt) "the look on his face" which became a standard phrase in our family when taking the piss.

And that was about it. Sadly I was too young to remember the pet monkey another aunt had, I know, not a dog, but hey, a pet monkey FFS! Different times eh?

I think my father's upbringing had included a dog, which I feel he hated, and that was probably why we were never allowed to have one at home. Although, perhaps it was more to do with thinking my mother would be incapable of looking after it on her own - that makes more sense! We were allowed, after serious negotiating by my sisters, to have a Hamster, not quite a dog but in the world of pets a first rung on the ladder to dogdom. I think he was a rescue, or someone had suggested they were going to put him down the toilet or similar, so my older sister, aided and abetted by my younger sister, managed to get our parents to agree that we could have him.

Petting time was strictly limited, I was third on the list of three, my parents not being in the least bit interested, but I did have the advantage of being home more than my sisters so I could sneak him out when they weren't there. I have two memories of "Monty" – the first was when I poked him to wake him up, I marvelled at his yellow incisors for a couple of nanoseconds before they made sharp contact with my fingers allowing blood to flow all over the place. Bastard rodent!

The second is really quite astonishing in view of the fact that my father apparently didn't like pets. Our back garden sloped upwards and my father, Mr Resource, had made two tiers of lawn with a path leading from the front of the first, uphill, obviously, and ending at the back of the second tier.

The tiers were separated by a wall which joined the path. The path was not as thick as the height of the wall so there was an area of earth beneath the path and adjacent to the end of the wall.

As you do, my sisters and I are walking "Monty", in the beautiful sunshine blessing our garden that day. "Monty" ever the adventurer (he could master stairs, 12 seconds his PB) or perhaps he had been in a

POW camp in a former life, decides to make a bid for freedom. The wheel and sunflower seeds clearly not enough for him in his hamsterian little life. Off he runs and manages to make it to the path-wall intersection. Shortly after that, straight out of "The Wooden Horse" he's tunnelling and disappearing, rapidly disappearing in fact, into the bowels of the upper lawn never to be seen again, or so we thought.

I've often tried to place myself in the shoes of my father on that day. Someone who admittedly liked a crisis, but also someone who was not adverse to going nuts at his offspring and spouse. As an example, I digress, sorry. Once we went to the Isle of Wight on holiday (1965, different times). I suspect my mother had been getting on his nerves during the ferry crossing and this resulted in him driving off the ferry, up the road about 500 yards, turning left, stopping the car and ordering us all to get out stating "You're not worth a ha'penny the lot of you." That got the holiday off to a great start. I mean what drove someone to do that?

Back to the back garden on that glorious day. What would you have done? I think I know what I would have done – I would have gone nuts at my children, said "too bad" and hoped that tunnelling Monty would retrace his excavations and return, together with some rare Anglo-Saxon gold ring and we could all rejoice etc., etc. Yes I feel that would have been the sensible option, adding a bit of how careless they were and that we would never have another pet, laying it on with a trowel, and watching them dissolve in tears. Oops, perhaps not so

10

harsh. But that is exactly what I would have expected my father to have done. Which he probably did…….but there was an addition to his rant.

He proceeded to dig up the lawn with a fork, I can still see the "dagger pointed hamster spearing tines" on it, all three of us watching as it punctured the green sward, all three of our hearts in our mouths hoping that, when it came out again, it hadn't pierced poor little Monty. Much to our relief and probably, incredibly to his surprise, not only did he not skewer Monty but he actually found him alive and well, but sadly lacking a Sutton Hoo helmet or similar – useless rodent.

I asked myself a question. Did my father actually like pets? If so why weren't we allowed a dog? He further confounded my original thoughts about him when in 1982 I returned home having finished university. In my final year I had won a goldfish at a local fair, which I had called Fido (Fucking Incredibly Dull Object) and when I moved out of the family home Fido stayed, my father assiduously looking after him, feeding and changing his water – I think he was heartbroken when he died. But not heartbroken enough to give Fido a full military style burial in the garden. He got the naval option….

My older sister married in 1971 and with her new husband, moved into their first property. Imagining the conversations that they had relating to what they needed for their flat, I would have been wrong to think chairs, table, cups, kettle and should, of course, put "DOG" at the top of the list. Yep, or yap, free from my father's dog curfew the first

11

thing she did was get a dog from the PDSA, Poor Dogs Salvation Army as she (and no doubt countless others) termed it. It is unlikely that the PDSA would have been looking after pedigrees, far more likely that the new arrival would be of the Heinz 57 variety which he was, but he came with a sort of pedigree, so she said – he was definitely a cross between a Foxhound and a Labrador. So he was. Not. My sister, in a slightly Hyacinth Bouquet moment, I suspect invented this story to avoid the word "mongrel" passing over her slightly snobby lips. And this was further enhanced by his name – "Waggy" - or "Wagstaff" as she insisted. What a great name, Waggy, and he was. His tail caught my accoutrements once, when I was in my pyjamas, men readers you know what it is like, female readers, you don't – eye watering – ouch, and always a slight delay after the impact before the pain comes, why is that?

Waggy is without doubt the best dog I have ever had the pleasure of meeting. Gloriously disobedient, you could see him run off, hear "Come here now!!!" watch him look back, weigh up the situation and think "Fuck off, I'm having too much fun." as he then turned and ran off into the distance, probably chasing a horse or similar. Funny, loving and with an incredible gastronomic taste too. I sat in the car with my newly born niece once and watched her puke up the entire contents of her stomach; the more she puked the more Waggy gobbled it all up – incredible creature. My sister lived next to a school and when Mr Whippy arrived, not a euphemism at this point in the story for a dog poo, he'd queue up with the school kids to get a broken cone with a bit of ice-cream on it. Free!

Her house was a few hundred yards away from where my parents lived and on several occasions he just turned up uninvited. "Went for a walk and thought I'd pop in for a drink," – he seemed to be saying - "Tea, lots of sugar, ta."

Like my uncle and Kimmy, my father and Waggy were great friends. My father idolised him too, giving him lots of (very bad) treats and he would make him tea, but he would only drink it if there was sugar in it. He would always sit under my father's chair in the living room, not sure how he squeezed in there but he always did. I can't help but think there was also a similarity in what Waggy did for my father. He wasn't suffering from mental health problems himself, that was my mother, but clearly that would have affected him, although he would never let it show, or admit to it – sad in retrospect. I think Waggy was a great diversion for him and he was more than happy to be kept in bad food and probably bad tea. The dog that is, although remembering my Mother's cooking it could equally apply to my Father. He was, though, a super dog and a brilliant companion. I loved it when he came to stay.

My favourite story about Waggy is early on in his career, before he had "his pockets picked" – castration, orchidectomy, choose one. Waggy was not averse to humping visitors, particularly nubile women, though men were fine too, he wasn't fussy, chair legs even offered light relief when no human flesh was available. However on this particular

13

evening plenty of human and non-human flesh was available. My sister and husband had invited both sets of parents over for drinks, I was invited too. My brother-in-law's mother *really was* Hyacinth Bouquet and spoke with a faux posh accent and went on lots of cruises, which back then were the height of luxury. My brother-in-law referred to her as the Duchess, cruel but fair. The Duke and Duchess arrived with the Duchess wearing a very expensive fur coat (different times).

Coats were removed and taken upstairs (an odd ritual in those days) and stilted conversation commenced. Shortly after, it was noticed that Waggy had gone AWOL and my sister called him. Thud, thud, thud announced his arrival and he ran round the room proudly showing something he had in his teeth.

"Oh what's the little devil got now." the Duchess asked.

"Come here now!" my sister shouted.

"Piss off, this tastes way too good." thought Waggy.

Eventually he was caught and the item removed. The item, as you will have guessed by now was part of the Duchess's fur coat. But there was worse to come – literally – he had really got it together with the coat, I'll leave that to your imagination, but think "removal and cleaning" as well as repair. The best bit was to come. When my sister took the expensive "Russian Sable" fur coat to be repaired the gentleman behind the counter declared that it was in fact the Aldi of the fur world, very cheap! The poor old Duchess, my sister never did tell her.

Sadly, Waggy got a bit bitey in his old age and had to be put down, I think I was at university by then so was spared their grieving, which didn't last long as straight away they got another dog – "It'll help the healing process." – looked rather disrespectful to me. "Ben" arrived, another H57 "spaniel-labrador" type thing. He was fun too, but I don't really remember too much about him. He got bitey too, although when being frequently at the wrong end of a rolled up newspaper wielded by my brother-in-law I guess it was not that surprising. Positive reinforcement wasn't known back then!

My sister had claimed that if she had a dog from a puppy, she would be able to train it beautifully. My nieces and brother-in-law decided to try her out and so "Nicky", a pedigree cocker spaniel, arrived following Ben's demise. "It'll help the healing process." The only things I concluded from seeing Nicky in action was a) my sister was lying and b) never ever get a spaniel. Nicky got farmed out eventually and hopefully led a lovely life wrecking someone else's house and garden.

My younger sister, not to be outdone had a dog called Shula. This was my wedding present, (it cost a 75p donation to the Blue Cross), to the happy couple (or not so happy as it turned out). Yet another "H57", she looked like a cross between a Fox and a dog. I only remember two things about her, firstly that she absolutely hated water and secondly that she laid a cable by my bed one night and I stepped in it the next morning when I woke up. This was a serious encounter with dog poo, something best avoided I noted to myself.

Happy memories, well mainly I guess, and I smile as I remember them. I don't remember seriously thinking I should get a dog, there was no need, I was in the perfect situation, if I wanted to satisfy any urge to be a dog owner I only needed to nip to either sister's house and it was done.

I do think I've always had a soft spot for dogs though, certainly when out bird watching I have always been happy, mostly, when dogs have come up to me; I hold out a hand for them to sniff and generally they are friendly. However the thought of owning one, back then, had completely disappeared, it simply wouldn't fit in with our lifestyle and there wasn't really anyone to look after a dog if we decided to go away, my parents having shuffled off their respective mortal coils, 391 days apart in the early '90s, and my wife's were in a different country.

But then the kids arrived and as those little bundles of joy grew older they formed a military alliance whose main objective was to conquer their parents' reluctance to "get a dawg". The pressure was mounting, even my wife, the Quisling, being involved sometimes. But I held firm, and imagined how "macho" my wife would think I was, standing up to this pressure. I think secretly she was pissed off that I wouldn't cave in, and worse still, that I had permanently ruined the children's lives.

As if!

Mind you our house wasn't a complete pet desert, we had had a cat, Zizi, (look it up on Google translate, it is a rude French word), a rabbit, guinea pigs, Fire-bellied newts, a hamster and fish in a pond and in a tank. Fish are therapeutic, as is a pond. It was with great delight that we were able to have one built in our garden, I loved it. I wasn't too keen on the local Grey Heron having a nose, well a beak actually, though.

Pondering on that thought - someone I worked with wanted to fill in their pond, sacrilege, and offered me about 10 massive carp, for free, well a bottle of gin. I transported them home in a large plastic box and to my surprise they all survived after a 40 mile car journey which saw them constantly stubbing their noses against the container I had put them in. They were fine, just a bit shorter.

Acclimatised, I released them and stood back with pleasure as they swam around in their new surroundings. Serenity personified, or piscinified if there is such a word. Fish don't need much looking after, less so in a pond, but I did feed them regularly with flakes, which I enjoyed as they seemed to come to the call – well it seemed that way.

One day, in a rush to get to a meeting, I went to feed them and saw that the flakes had congealed into a little ball. "Oh well, big feed for them." I thought as I tossed it in the pond. I arrived home late and went straight to bed. Refreshed, I woke up, opened the curtains and saw what looked like an apocalypse, a mass of floating carp – dead, obviously. Clearly I had poisoned them and apart from feeling awful, wondered how I had done so. A quick bit of research found that the huge mass of flakes had probably resulted in a large rush of ammonia released in the pond, which deprived them of their oxygen – what an awful death, 'suffocation' I guess. Not all of them died, the smaller ones seemed to survive and one largish one. But eventually he, or she, succumbed. I decided to put it out of its misery, but could not bring myself to hit it with a heavy object, so shot it with an air rifle from my bedroom window. Blood began to seep out into the pond, so I had to run downstairs, fish it out of the pond and despatch it finally, with another pellet. I felt really bad about all this, and remembering it now, probably 10 or more years later I still feel guilty, those poor fish.

After the members of the menagerie had all gone to meet their makers, we acquired another cat, Todd. Todd features later, but Todd is a git, remember that. But we had not caved into the pressure and got a dog. And I was determined not to have one, whereas the others had an opposite view. When the subject came up for discussion, I vehemently defended my corner with these brilliant discussion points:

"Who looks after it during the day?" – feel guilty, animal cruelty purveyors.

"Who is going to pick up the poo?" – sheepish looks all round.

"Where does it go when we go on holiday?" – shock of no more holidays.

I was winning and then the real *"coup de grace"* was wrong footing them by saying that we could have a dog if we could find one that satisfied two simple rules. The kids were shocked, I think my wife was too. Were we really going to get a dog? The rules were:

It must not bark.

It must not poo.

They hated me! Although in fairness a Basenji just about satisfies number 1, but ho, ho, it does number 2s so doesn't satisfy number 2. So apart from being a not bad word in Scrabble, Basenji doesn't work and besides Viszler scores more for the same number of letters. Actually Scrabble wouldn't be a bad name for a dog would it?

Time marched on and the kids grew up and having a dog became less of a priority. Todd did go some way to being a dog, well not really I just made that up, but X-Box, WhatsApp, FaceBook, drinking, partying, and university were the real substitutes and that was just me! Owning a dog dissolved into the background of everyday life and with both of us still working full-time, the idea was forgotten thank goodness…...or was it?

A year or two later and my daughter has a new boyfriend who, would you believe it, has a dog. This is "Jack" an H57 Jack Russell x Border Terrier (I've got into the terminology with the "x" for cross – oooh get me).

"Can he bring Jack to the house please?"

Something stirred inside me. I desperately wanted to say "No", for fear of the dog argument rising up again and of course Todd would have his "arrogant little shit" nose put out. But I found myself feeling a frisson of excitement and without any discussion with my wife blurted out:

"Of course he can – look forward to it."

I can imagine my daughter thinking to herself "Eh? What's going on here?" I couldn't deny it, I was very excited, this could be a very useful exercise, I couldn't wait. Jack came, barked and shat all over the garden and then left, he was happy!

THE TRIAL PART ONE

Here we are some 40 years on from Waggy, and after our introduction to "Barking Shitting Jack" (BSJ) my daughter asks us if we would be prepared to look after him for a whole weekend. My first thought is that I will not be the one picking up the poo. My second thought is I might need to buy some ear-defenders and my final thought is that, hmmm, this might be just what I am looking for....taking a dog for a real test drive. It seemed a bit crazy as we had virtually no experience of dogs on our own, but with our son also ensconced at university and the fact that the two of us were rattling around at home, which in subtext means getting on each other's tits, it seemed like a rather good, jolly jape. When BSJ arrived I was reminded of having young children again.

"This is his crate, he sleeps here at night, this is his bed, he sleeps here during the day, this is his food, only feed him twice a day, here are some treats, don't give him too many, and these are only if he is really good, but if he is exceptionally good then give him this chew, this is his lead, this is a spare lead, here are some poo bags (they went straight in my wife's pocket), here are his toys, this is his favourite, but these other 2 million will keep him happy, he needs to be let out every so often for a pee and he'll do a poo in the morning then probably one in the evening, but if he gets excited he might do one in the day too – think that's it, thanks, love you."

I had imagined a car pulling up, BSJ getting out, B-ing and S-ing, we'd be given some sort of restraining device, a collar and a lead as I remembered it back in the 1970s, and some food. It was like some massive project and he was only staying two nights. Blinkin' flip. One sort of positive point, if you can say that, was that after unloading the articulated lorry, the two of us no longer rattled around, in fact it was a bit of a challenge to find any space – BSJ had taken over.

Daughter and boyfriend departed and we were 'on our own' – arggh what to do? Just like having a new born in the house. Okay out to the garden…

"Come on Jack!"

He looked quizzically at me, cocked his little head and then ran after me. He really was quite sweet, although when he ran it looked as if he had had his head put in a vice and twisted relative to his spine – he looked a bit odd, but apparently this was normal Jack. Out in the garden in March, for a change, it was sunny and BSJ was very happy, so happy the first thing he did was a territorial shit and when I held up a ball he barked – the eponymous BSJ. Bark, bark, bark, bark, "Shut the fuck up you twat." I said, which fell on deaf ears. Well not deaf ears but he obviously didn't understand it, I might just as well have said "There's a sale on at IKEA." or "dsfh dfidfh idfsuklfae oefihlskjan slfnlk." In anger I threw the ball away and lo and behold he stopped barking – brilliant. Off he trotted, head on the slant, and picked the ball up, turned round and came bounding back.

"Drop it!" I offered.

22

He was having none of this and so began a procession of trying to grab him, to get the ball, a sort of canine version of 'He'. Jack was way too smart, distraction didn't work either. After a while though, I managed to grab him and quickly realised that he had no idea about finesse when it came to controlling his bite. Eventually I prised the ball out of his mouth, counted my fingers, all present and correct, success? No. The moment there was no contact between the ball and BSJ's gob he started barking. And it wasn't a sort of bark that you could put up with, it was a "Yap, yap, yap." that just went through me along the lines of someone running their nails down a blackboard. I threw the ball away quickly – silence, quickly followed by "He", followed by finger counting, followed by yap.

Throw.

He.

Fingers.

Yap,yap,yap,yap,yap,yap,yap,yap,yap,yap,yap,yap,yap,yap,yap,yap, yap,yap,yap,yap,yap,yap,yap,yap,yap,yap,yap,yap,yap,yap,yap,yap, yap,yap,yap,yap,yap,yap,yap,yap,yap,yap,yap,yap,yap,yap,yap,yap.

Throw.

He.

Fingers.

Yap,yap,yap,yap,yap,yap,yap,yap,yap,yap,yap,yap,yap,yap,yap,yap, yap,yap,yap,yap,yap,yap,yap,yap,yap,yap,yap,yap,yap,yap,yap,yap, yap,yap,yap,yap,yap,yap,yap,yap,yap,yap,yap,yap,yap,yap,yap,yap.

Throw.

He.

Fingers.

Yap,yap,yap,yap,yap,yap,yap,yap,yap,yap,yap,yap,yap,yap,yap,yap,yap,
yap,yap,yap,yap,yap,yap,yap,yap,yap,yap,yap,yap,yap,yap,yap,yap,yap,
yap,yap,yap,yap,yap,yap,yap,yap,yap,yap,yap,yap,yap,yap,yap,yap,yap.
Throw.

He.

Fingers.

Yap,yap,yap,yap,yap,yap,yap,yap,yap,yap,yap,yap,yap,yap,yap,yap,yap,
yap,yap,yap,yap,yap,yap,yap,yap,yap,yap,yap,yap,yap,yap,yap,yap,yap,
yap,yap,yap,yap,yap,yap,yap,yap,yap,yap,yap,yap,yap,yap,yap,yap,yap.
My ears could take no more so we went back inside.

"Did you have fun?" my wife asked

"Um."

"Oh look at his little face, his tail wagging, I'll take him back in the garden."

It was a little bit of a result, there was no "Throw", no "He" and no "Fingers" but no matter where I went in the rattleless house, I could still hear that bloody "Yap, yap, yap.", I went shopping for some beers.

THE TRIAL PART TWO

BSJ eventually got bored of Throw, He, Fingers and came back inside. After a quick slurp of water he crashed out on his bed (the day bed not the night bed) and that was it for the day......or so I thought. The beers I had bought were slipping down nicely when I was told that "He needs to go for a walk to do a wee." This really annoyed me, but shamed into it, by stories my wife concocted about being abducted by some thug as she walked along the roads nearby, I reluctantly left Stella and went out. BSJ kept us waiting but after about 10 minutes finally emptied his bladder and we could all return home.

In the sport of crashing out, BSJ was a master, back from a wee, again he crashed out, but this time in his crate, and it was, as Zebedee might have said (that's just for older readers folks), "Time for bed." Hoorah!

The next morning dawned and we had heard nothing from BSJ all night. This was, initially, good news. This good news was soon replaced by the dreadful thought that, as amateur dog sitters, BSJ had either escaped or snuffed it during the night. We both rushed downstairs but fortunately BSJ was fine, wagging his tail and cocking his head. He looked so sweet when he wasn't outside annoying the world. We decided to take him for a decent walk and loaded him up in the car. He clearly knew the routine here, wagging his tail and not making a sound even though he chose to squash himself in front of the front seat. He couldn't see anything and I thought he must surely puke up – but he didn't. Perhaps he had something wrong with his ears?

The walk was in a forest not far from our house, with a lovely lake which, the main reason for the choice, normally hosted some Mandarin ducks. (As a very keen, but crap, birdwatcher I was looking for what are termed 'year-ticks' – birds that you have not seen in that calendar year so far). With the car parked, I ticked Mandarin straight away, with a bonus Goosander, and that done, the proper walk could commence. Along the wooded track (Marsh Tit, another year tick), out to the open heath, across the stream and there we were, out in the beautiful countryside with BSJ running around all over the place. He absolutely loved it.

"Here Jack."

" Come on good, boy."

"Jaaaaackkkkk, heeeeeerrrrre."

"Jack you little shit, get here now!!"

BSJ was having none of it, having slipped the surly bonds of his lead he was not going to miss out on this unfettered opportunity to roam around, jump in gorse bushes, chase imaginary creatures through bracken and eat tons of horse poo – he seemed to like it more than his normal food.

Eventually he came back, much to our relief, but, after giving him a treat for returning, he was off again, supplementing this *"amuse-bouche"* with a horse turd main course – yummy. And of course he was no mug.

26

"If I run off and worry them I get a treat." he thought – peeeoooowwwww – off he zapped, well as zappy as he could be with his stumpy little form, behind a gorse bush and firmly out of sight.

"Jack." dulcet tones.

"Jack." slightly stronger tones.

"Jack." slightly stronger than above with hint of panic.

"JACK!!!!!!!!" full scale panic.

Jack knew what was going on, he was running his "CJ from Reggie Perrin" app:

"One, two, three, four - make 'em wait outside the door. Five, six, seven, eight - always pays to make 'em wait. Nine, ten, eleven, twelve - come!

Lovely, yet another fishy treat. What a piece of piss and what a couple of mugs!

We walked miles but BSJ's energy seemed unstoppable, he just ran and ran and ran. And it was great fun. I was enjoying it (for a start I was three up on my year bird list) and watched him enjoying himself too.

The light began to fade and so we headed back to the car. We'd brought water, which was completely ignored, ungrateful git, and then he happily jumped in the car and fell asleep until we got home. At home he was happy to lay on his bed for the rest of the evening – result! Time for beers – what a lovely day – "He needs a walk so he can have a wee." Groundhog day again. Off we went around the block again and he dutifully did his business. Back at home, I resumed my alcoholic activities, now onto red wine, and reflected on the day.

27

Overall it was pretty enjoyable, but there were a couple of "burrs on the saddle" – the reality that a dog might need a lot of looking after, and obviously BSJ was at the "not much looking after needed" end of the spectrum, and the requirement for "pee-walks" interrupting my enjoyment of alcohol. Hmm, tricky. I wasn't convinced. I was way too selfish.

My wife loved it, and was convinced. However the full-time jobs were really the blocker here. We could have a dog and just leave it during the day, or get one of those professional dog-walkers to help, or farm it out to friends, but this was no life and seemed grossly unfair. No, if we were to have one then we would have to commit to looking after it properly, "pee walk" included.

I reflected some more. It wasn't that I didn't want a dog, it was more to do with the realisation that it was a "24/7" thing, rather than an "Oh that's nice now get back in the cupboard." thing. Deep down I knew I wanted a dog, but the jobs gave a convenient way of dismissing the idea without having to worry too much about it.

We discussed "What if we did this?" and "How about that?" and "Could so and so do that perhaps?" It was never going to happen. – or was it?

JINGLE BELLS

Like a tattoo, a dog is for life, not just for Christmas. With both of us still in full-time jobs it might be a little awkward, dog sitting, but I was sure it could be done, couldn't it? After all it can't be that difficult, can it?

There had been much furtive stuff going on in the lead up to Christmas. I recognised the deliberate clues, hushed tones, texting, PC screens being diverted as I walked into a room – mind you it could have been my teenage son was watching porn. No, it couldn't be that surely? No, my inner canine was fully alerted and ready to go, yes it had to be 'the big secret' coming to life – at last. What a Christmas to remember.....

I'll be honest, I was somewhat apprehensive, yet excited too – would it be a miniature Schnauzer (lovely) a Border Terrier (sweet) or.....well in my mind those were the only options, so anything outside that box would be something of a disappointment. Hiding my disappointment is not one of my core competencies, so I would have to do my best acting if a bloody Labrador jumped out of that same box on 25th December.

Christmas Eve came and *"en-famille"* we ended up going to Midnight Mass (well the "just before Midnight Mass", the JBM Mass), we are not religious (bet you didn't see that revelation coming), so it's probably hypocritical, but I like the "Christmas tunes" and the architecture of churches is interesting. And there is a general bonhomie inside – candles everywhere (what's not to like about candles?) nice scents normally but, as it was pissing down outside, a general dank smell pervaded the congregation.

As I checked my watch, and realised that it was only a minute since the last time I checked it, a horrid thought crossed my mind. In the background the Vicar was talking about God, Jesus, mankind and Lego (to encourage the younger amongst us) but "Why are we here at all?" I mused? This was not me suddenly becoming a Yuletide Philosopher, but me wondering why, if there was a puppy lurking at home, were we here in the Church at just before Midnight Mass? Why were we not within barking or whimpering distance, in case it was lonely, cold and worried? I imagined the poor waif all alone, probably heartbroken and so scared that it had made its own Midnight Mess. Suddenly, in a minor epiphany, it struck me that 'dog' was in fact an anagram of 'God' – ironically it was almost a religious experience – spooky - the signs were clearly there then – coincidence? Nah. My heart skipped a beat.

Cocktail party syndrome kicked in and I drifted back into the JBM Mass, when I heard "wine and bread" mentioned, but sadly it was for the chosen few who'd been 'done' earlier in their wonderful lives. I felt it rather unchristian to be excluded, yet I knew I could not join the conga and fake it (the Vicar knew me), so I drifted off into the canine cosmos. The JBM Mass turned out to be a largely charmless hour of boredom with a load of chanting about "Glory to God". I silently chanted "Glory to Dog" and instead spent a while contemplating how

30

I'd cope with pooing? By this I meant picking up the dog's poo, not my own constitution, which was fine by all accounts, despite the excitement.

But the whole reverie worried me. My wife and kids, clearly, were not in the top league of animal husbandry if the poor thing was on its own somewhere at home. In the garage, in the shed, in the microwave? Were they that cruel, or that stupid? Surely not, my daughter was hoping to study to become a Vet so she should know about such things for sure. My Dog, I mean God, perhaps I had had a massive bout of confirmation bias and all the "clues" were nothing of the sort and there was no God, I mean Dog.

Really?

The JBM Mass over, the masses left and wended their way back to their houses – it was just past midnight, so officially Christmas Day. We arrived home and decided to open a present each – something that we had never done before. Aha, here we go..........puppy incoming, he needs feeding!!

Socks. Fucking socks.

Wine, bed, snoring, dreaming 'Sit!', 'Heel!', 'Good dog!', bladder calls, up awake, can't go back to sleep, drift off and then it's time to wake up - groan. Our children were, thankfully, past the age of waking up before they went to bed on Christmas Day but there was still a ritual (which still exists to this day!) of them coming into our bedroom with a sackful of "little presents" which my wife had carefully chosen on one

31

of her expeditions to the "Shops of Tat" which pop up at this time of year. All carefully wrapped, all gratefully received. All very nice but......this ritual took about 30 minutes, and I really began to think it was the height of cruelty. How could they keep ME in suspense for so long? That poor puppy unless.............oh yes here we go, a car pulled up outside. Door slammed shut, boot slammed shut.

"Okay, let's go downstairs and open up the proper presents."

Yayyyy, puppy incoming, literally.

Off we went, yet there was no doorbell – odd. Under the tree in the lounge were the "proper presents", none of them dog shaped, none of them moving, none of them making a dog like noise. That was disappointing. No smell of poo or pee either, that wasn't disappointing but it was worrying, if you see what I mean.

"Here's your pile." my wife said, thrusting a tower of presents towards me.

Call me Mr Picky, but the stack looked suspiciously like books, clothes, some Tat and more fucking socks. And it was! In the end to avoid bursting I asked:

"Okay so where is it?"

"Where's what?"

"The puppy you've been hiding from me for the last few days."

A collective "Eh?" echoed around the lounge.

"Don't be daft, we haven't bought a puppy – how on earth could you look after it, there's nobody here during the day."

And that was it, I was let down like a cheap pair of braces – no puppy, no picking up poo to consider. I was a broken man.

I got dressed, new fucking socks pulled on, turned the oven on and cooked some bacon and sausages, poured a stiff G+T and decided that, as usual, I bloody hated Christmas.

A YEAR LATER

I haven't seen the film "Groundhog Day" but I have a vague idea of what it is about – being trapped in a time-loop and similarly here I am a year later…....

There had been much furtive stuff going on in the lead up to Christmas. I recognised the deliberate clues, hushed tones, texting, PC screens being diverted as I walked into a room.......but we've swapped JBM Mass for "Carols in the Square" in a village a few miles away. This immediately gets my vote as it is much earlier in the evening and, and, oh, I see!!! Much earlier in the evening eh? This is clearly a puppy fuelled change to our normal activities because, of course, the puppy needs to be in place at a reasonable time. Midnight Mass might affect its routine so sneaking it into the house earlier, or perhaps delivering it earlier is much kinder. Of course!

We have a few drinks and dinner, which is lovely and with artificial snow blowing all over the place I am beginning to get into this Christmas lark. We arrive home at a much more reasonable hour. I am expecting to be told to stay up past midnight, for obvious confirmation bias reasons, but strangely everyone else appears to be "tired and emotional" and soon they disappear up the stairs to the land of nod. I stay in the lounge and can't help but think I have yet again fooled myself into thinking I am shortly to be a proud dog owner.

Midnight comes and goes, nobody rushes downstairs and shouts 'Ha ha fooled you, look at this little wonder' – so I finish my glass of

34

wine and begin to trudge upstairs. The cat comes to say a festive "Merry Christmas." and I reply, seasonally, with "Fuck off you Ginger Whinger." – Bah humbug!

The next day, well you can guess, socks................I bloody hate Christmas.

A YEAR LATER

Don't just don't go there okay?

It didn't happen, it was never going to happen, I wanted a dog, I had never had a dog.

Get over it.

I did, but I did wonder if one day it might happen?

PART 2

DAVID GILMOUR AND ROGER WATERS

I am staring at a wall, and I am feeling uncomfortably numb (did you see what I did there?). Sadly, there isn't going to be a soaring guitar solo shortly but my earworm for the day is going to be a funeral march, moving on to a requiem (hopefully Ravel's if there has to be one) later.

The wall I am staring at is a wall of text, all 1200 words of it – I used that function to count because I was so stunned at the verbosity of it. A few weeks earlier I had had a "6 month review" (objectives update etc) with my boss. It wasn't dreadful, not at all, it wasn't brilliant either, but I walked out of the office thinking all was okay, let's get on with all the stuff we need to do. My boss did bring up, yet again, the fact that I had made some criticism of her style; come on who wouldn't criticise a micro-managing control freak, who, despite telling everyone else to "pick up the phone and let's talk" still communicated largely by large, long e-mails. If only I had known the phrase "tldr" back then!

I admit that I could have delivered the criticism a bit better for sure, and it would no doubt have helped had my colleague, who agreed we needed to explain how we felt, hadn't suddenly become all chocolate fire-guardy and mute. But it was all smiles as we each went our way and nothing more was said, until about 3 weeks later when the email arrived which started:

'Sorry I have only just written up the notes from our meeting....'.

I had completely forgotten about that meeting and initially just read the email cursorily, the normal things "do this" "make sure this is done by such and such a date", "go and see so and so" "get this exhibition prepared". Some things stood out, inaccuracies, injustices, or lies might be a better term. I was a bit taken aback. A criticism for something that I had not done in the previous year, yet I distinctly remembered asking whether it was a problem if it was not completed and being told "No, not at all." The more I read the more I got angry and then, "bingo!" I re-read it carefully and watched as my mouse morphed into a scorpion. For there right in front of me was a very nasty sting in the tail, or a veiled threat as people would call it.

"We will meet again in a couple of months and if the above and attached have not been completed to the correct standard then we will discuss this in a more formal way."

Uh-oh, this is performance managing me out of the business. I was truly shocked. I had worked my arse off for this company although I did notice that nothing was ever quite good enough, so I am not sure why I was shocked. If you do a crap job and get criticised then, in my opinion, the criticism is easier and fairer to take. If you genuinely felt you did a good job and were still criticised, well that is tough to take, and that is where I was at that moment.

I broke down.

It was the straw that broke a weak camel's back. The day before, in a massive proud parent moment, I had seen my daughter sign the Royal College of Veterinary Science register as she qualified as a Veterinary

39

Surgeon, and here I was a blubbing wreck – talk about bathos, Shakespeare would have been pissing himself.

I called my wife, bless her, she came home to console me. She probably thought it totally ridiculous, totally spineless, but I really was a broken man. I called my boss's boss (someone I had known for 30 years who originally worked for me back then, and the person who invited me to apply for this position – he then got promoted hence I had a new boss) which was not good protocol but by then I thought "Fuck it who cares?" I held it together for about 1 minute then burst into tears again. God it was awful, embarrassing, but I simply could not control myself. Within a few minutes I had pressed "Send" and resigned. All I had to look forward to was a 3 months' notice period.

But every cloud has a silverish lining and a meeting was called to sort out what actually needed to be done in those 3 months, or so I thought. I had a holiday booked right at the end of the notice period but not enough remaining holiday to avoid making a return to work afterwards. My big negotiating tactic was to get an extra day off so that I didn't have to return, that would have been horrid. As it happened I didn't need my great negotiator's hat on as, straight away, I was told that I could go within a week.

"There's nothing you do that we can't do between us." my ex-apprentice said, perhaps not realising that this was one of the unkindest things he had ever said in his life.

40

I felt totally worthless, but still put on a poker face and said concernedly, "But there's stuff I want to finish." – fortunately my inner Pinocchio kept quiet and I "reluctantly" agreed to go.

What a result!!! Mind you my paranoia did give me a hard time as to whether they had someone already lined up to replace me (apparently not). Anyway, it was all over, but not before I received another e-mail of gargantuan proportions, which probably held the record for the most hyperlinks to the company's intranet, as it asked me to put "All of my excellent work." in various locations - I mean FFS how disingenuous was that comment? This completed, I met up with my boss's boss to hand over my 'phone and laptop and that was it. My proper boss didn't even bother to "pick up the phone" and call, such irony, WhatsApp or text. Even if she had said "good riddance" it would at least have been something! I expect she was delighted that a long e-mail resulted in my resignation – what a result!!!

After 36 and a bit years my career had seemingly come to an end. I wasn't sure if I was unemployed, unemployable, semi-retired or retired, or just plain pissed off. Probably the latter.

I had always craved retiring, and ironically, I had planned to do just that about 6 months after the time I was paid up to. So in truth, painful though it was, it was not going to be the end of the world. I was hurt even though I made the decision to resign, it wasn't really on my terms, I felt I had to. I could not face two months of being spied upon (I had had a session of that the year before) – but it did feel like constructive dismissal, it certainly didn't feel like retirement – for a start I felt incredibly guilty, and incredibly useless. My craving was misplaced, more confirmation bias no doubt.

What to do?

It was Friday, the pub beckoned, and we sat outside in the lovely evening sun with the river flowing past, making the world seem a decent place after all.

"Are you going to try and get another job?" my wife asked.

"There's a few things I could apply for but I can't face staying in the same industry now. Also, if I completely clamp down on "living expenses" I reckon I can survive with the pension I can take."

"Really?"

"Yes, it might be a bit tight, no big forays on Amazon or eBay, but I think I could do it."

"Hmm, well see what happens, don't panic."

With the Hitchhiker's Guide to the Galaxy's advice ringing in my ears I watched as a Kingfisher flashed past, all iridescence, the Halcyon of ancient Greece. Was it a portent that halcyon days were ahead?

I said "We could get a dog now, I'll be home all the time."

A GATE TO NATURE IS A GATE TO HEAVEN

Somewhere, not a million miles away from that pub, about the same time of year, Maisey woke up and felt 'odd'. She'd never felt like this before, what was it? Winston, not far away felt something too. He stood up, stretched his legs and without thinking started to walk towards her. He just couldn't stop himself, what was going on?

Maisey and Winston were a slightly odd couple. Those that knew them well said it would never last. In fact they had been good friends all along, there was nothing in the least bit romantic between them. Just good friends. They said. To everyone. And they were. Maisey liked Winston very much. Winston liked Maisey very much. But in the background there was the spectre of youth versus adulthood. The inevitable change from being young, without a care in the world, to a world with taxes and death – the only two things you can be sure of in life other than England never winning the World Cup again.

Winston couldn't work out this feeling, he thought to himself

> *"But soft, what light through yonder window breaks?*
> *It is the east, and Maisey is the sun."*

Meanwhile Maisey was distraught

> *"O Winston, Winston,*
> *wherefore art thou Winston?*

Deny thy father and refuse thy name,
Or if thou wilt not, be but sworn my love,
And I'll no longer be just a Springer Spaniel."

Oh dear. Pheromones. Yum. Pheromones. Yum. Winston's "light through yonder window" was in fact the hall light streaming in through a baby gate. Beyond the gate Maisey stood tail wagging, beguiling, giving off a scent so powerful and irresistible that if it had been attractive to humans Coco Chanel would've patented it. Winston sniffed and sniffed and sniffed. He paced round and round and round, clockwise, anticlockwise, straight ahead, then left, then right ad nauseum until he couldn't take any more. But the baby gate had other ideas. It was the perfect foil to Maisey's allure and Winston's drive. Well thought out by their owners before they left for an evening out, leaving a randy cur with an on-heat bitch required precautions. Sensible.

"None of that stuff you two eh?"

Winston was a Cockapoo, he wasn't huge but he was keen. Their eyes met, their noses touched, coyly she backed away. His snout went further and further towards her until......graunnnnnnnchhhh.

"Bollocks." he said to himself in Dogian

He was now jammed in the baby gate. "Grrrnnnnnthh" he said as he pushed his paws against the bar and removed himself. There then followed several minutes of overt stupidity as Winston continued his hopeless routine, pace, pace, jam, remove, pace, pace, jam, remove. In the end he began to tire so curled up on the floor, head on paws, staring at Maisey, who by this time was pretty unimpressed and getting more desperate by the second. Her hormones continued to course through her body "Here I am, come and get me." they messaged like some canine Bluepaw.

Winston knew he had to up his game and change tack, but how? He went to the gate and put his paws on the top and started jumping. Maisey got excited. But it was all in vain. Eventually he realised this wouldn't work. Back to lying down head on paws. A massive waft of pheromones entered his nose. This was it, this was the motivation, this was his "elixir". He walked backwards, sizing up the gate and then suddenly he ran full pelt at the gate. Just before he reached it he leapt in the air and caught his bollocks on the top and fell back on the carpet. Maisey, in a dog way, pissed herself laughing. "Woof, woof" which translated as "You useless cretin get a grip and mind your tackle."

Licking his "tarnished testicles", (because he can chaps, because he can) he was soon ready for a second leap of faith. And this time he did it, and landed in a heap on Maisey. Both parties were pleased and congress took place unbeknown to everyone except themselves and possibly every other male dog for 5 miles around.

Lying side by side on the floor, Winston lit a cigarette, put a paw behind his head and blew out a long plume of smoke. Turning to Maisey he said:

"Never in the field of canine coupling was so much sowed to a Springer by a Cockapoo.".

She looked back at him doe-eyed and said "You really are a nob Winston".

The owners arrived on the "crime" scene, Sherlock wouldn't have been troubled, it was obvious who the perpetrators were and what had occurred. And that was that, it was all over bar the counting.......

THE CIRCLE OF LIFE PART 1

"Well we don't know for sure do we?"

"I think we do."

"What if he's a canine Jaffa?"

"Eh?"

"You know, seedless."

"Unlikely."

"Just a straw clutcher."

THE CIRCLE OF LIFE PART 2

"Is it me or has Maisey put on weight?"

"Does a bear shit in the woods?"

"Holy moly, what are we going to do?"

TICKET TO SKIVE

I woke up the next morning, a Saturday, feeling slightly worse for wear thanks to a beer and red wine fuelled end to the evening. As I lay in bed, pretending to be asleep, so I didn't have to get up to feed the bastard cat Todd, I pondered and revisited my current plight. There were several options:

Get another job in the same industry with the products I knew – no, definitely not. I had done that once before and it was like playing football for *[enter your favourite team here]* and then being transferred to *[enter a team well below your favourite team]*, because I dropped the premier product for a not so good one. Yet I still had to tell my customers how good it was, even though I knew it wasn't - tough gig that is, believe me. No, not doing that again.

Get another job in a similar industry – hmm, tricky as up against people with a lot of experience, but.......an option.

Get another job in an industry that I knew nothing about – hmm see above for the answer.

Do nothing – that'll do!

But would it?

I spent the first few weeks not doing much, it was summer, there was the Cricket World Cup and the Ashes to entertain me, which they both did in bucketfuls, and the weather was pretty decent. There were hobbies I could do, bird watching, a bit of mild plane-spotting from the garden, crosswords, quizzes, su-doku, kakuro, karaoke, knitting (not really those last two, I just liked the alliteration), music – "Aha," I could learn some more piano pieces, improve my guitar playing, become a rock God! Or I could do something like some decorating or some gardening. Or perhaps I could even apply for some jobs!

My first port of call was an internet site I had used before, a specialist site for the industry I was in. I entered some keywords – "location", "salary", "sales" "marketing" and a load of completely irrelevant jobs came up – some filters are so crap – but once I had sifted through them I looked in more detail. There seemed to be a few I could apply for, some I even got vaguely excited about. I dashed off a few CVs with covering e-mails, and with all that excitement and tea drinking, a necessity for surfing for employment, I realised I needed to satisfy a call of nature. I went into the bathroom and while washing my hands looked at myself in the mirror, 60, fat, balding, and thought "Who the fuck is going to believe what I say or buy anything off me?"

I got used to the rejections, (I had had some good practice a few weeks before!), the first one hurt a bit though as I thought I was well qualified for that position. After a while I only had to see the e-mail to realise that I was not going to get any further along those primrose-lined roads. Despite the best intentions in the world of HR it is still hopelessly biased against old 'uns. It isn't experience companies crave, it's compliance.

In the end I simply gave up, or at least lessened my job hunting until it didn't really exist. This gave rise to many happy hours creating a "life" spreadsheet to see if I really could exist on the pension I had decided to take.

What I hadn't considered though, was the non-financial existence. Sometimes I thought "I'm retired, I can do all those things I want to do", but it never felt like that. And to be honest, although I had quite a few hobbies I did get a bit bored, for two reasons. One was the obvious one, that there's only so much of a hobby or interest you can take (or I can take perhaps) and secondly, much more importantly as I found out, you really need someone to share your retirement with.

It's particularly a problem if one of you is working:

"Hello how was your day?"

"I went out bird watching it was fab."

"And how was yours?"

"I stared at a computer screen for 8 hours without a break."

That awful imbalance hit me hard. Even though I had been the major earner for most of our life together (not forgetting that my wife also did the lioness's share of bringing up our kids), it made me feel so bad that she now had a bit of a sword of Damocles over her head, hopefully the thread would stay intact.

For those of you who have not "worked from home" believe me it is not a lot of fun, in fact I hated it, and I worked from home a lot. With only the cat to talk to, or to kick, when things weren't going well (I jest), it can be pretty soul destroying. I was quite good at being self-disciplined but would happily bugger off downstairs and play the piano for a while – justifying it as a tea break or looking for inspiration. If only. So "not working from home" had some advantage in that there was less guilt; I didn't have to skive, but in truth it was far more boring, only a handful of e-mails per day instead of 150+.

IT'S ALL OVER BAR THE COUNTING

One.

Two.

Three.

Four.

Five.

Six.

Seven.

Eight.

Nine.

Ten.

"Bloody hell ten! Maisey that is incredible, Winston, didn't know you had it in you, you little devil."

"Better get some puppy food."

"Kitchen roll and floor cleaner might be more of a priority!"

"OMFG!"

"Yes, OMFG!"

QUIZZICAL

I lay in bed one morning idly trying to remember the 50 states of the USA, I got 49, Nebraska I hate you, when I decided to pass the time by trying a "Which dog is suitable for you?" quiz. I answered the questions honestly and then somewhere in a maze of 'clickbait' I saw the horrific word:

CHIHUAHUA

What the actual fuck?!!

Arggh! I tried again and got Cairn Terrier or similar – no, no, no, where was Miniature Schnauzer or Border Terrier? I dismissed it as rubbish and canine thoughts disappeared once again...............or at least they did until I got a text from my daughter.

"Look I found u a puppy LOL."

There was a link which I ignored for a while. And then curiosity got the better of me so I clicked on it. The contact details were a mobile phone, so I immediately discounted that as a puppy farm. The directions would probably be to a service station on the M25 and the people would turn up in a black BMW with the windows blacked out. My daughter said I was being ridiculous. She went on saying that most people gave only their mobile phone numbers these days. I wasn't convinced but read a bit more.....

In the discussions we had had about having a dog, obviously the question of which breed had come up. Fortunately neither of us wanted a Chihuahua (sorry if you have them and love them) but there was quite a bit of disagreement on the choice. As you know I wanted a smallish dog, my wife wanted something like a Labrador and, to make matters worse, wanted a brown one? A brown Labrador? God I hated those, quite liked black ones, but too big.

On and on the debate went and it was ironically Pavlovian in its content:

Me: "How about a *[insert breed]* ?"

My wife: "No, don't like those."

My wife: "But how about a *[insert breed but not the same as above]*?"

Me: "No, don't like those."

We did agree that a dog that didn't shed its hair everywhere would be good, and our "research" suggested that Cockapoos were quite good in that regard and they were also relatively small and often not brown. I looked at some pictures of them, not bad actually– someone we knew had a black Cockapoo, he was okay I must admit. My wife wasn't overly convinced but we were perhaps moving towards a mutually agreeable target.

We went off to a garden centre to waste some money on overpriced crap and have a cup of tea and a slice of cake. While we were there I espied a massive stone statue of a dog. I photographed it and sent it to our kids with the caption "We've got a dog at last." There was some minor belief, that the event had happened, followed by much derision. Finishing the lovely scones I said:

55

"Shall I ring those people in the link?"

"Up to you."

I waited a few days before having a good discussion with myself about it. What would it be like having a dog? The responsibility, yikes, but then the walks with it, the bird watching I could do, oh no picking up poo, the fun it would be to train it, to see it grow up, to throw a ball, go to the seaside, to the local park. Of course it would need at least one walk a day. I then had another very serious discussion with myself saying that it was not possible to have a dog because it required a lot of looking after and someone needed to be at home. And someone needed to be at home. And someone needed to be at home. BINGO!!!! This dog was going to be my retirement ticket – what a result!!! I could look after him, and perhaps get a part-time job, or perhaps not get a job at all and I wouldn't need to feel guilty about it. Yayyy!

Our daughter had provided us with a long list of questions in order to vet the breeders (that's what Vets are for ho, ho). Gingerly I picked up my mobile, put the caller ID to off and dialled the number. I expected it to be a little like calling about a car for sale:

"Yeah mate it's on a 19 plate, brand new chip, full service, four good legs, automatic transmission, and low emissions." that would have been such a lie.

Instead it was far more jovial and pleasant. I explained that my daughter was a Vet and there were a lot of questions to ask and did she mind if I went through them all. That wouldn't be a problem and so I ploughed on with the 'interview' and all seemed fine, although I did baulk at the price – that was like a used car.

I sent the feedback to our daughter and that all added up, so just waited for my wife to arrive home:

"How was your day?"

"Yes not too bad, only 5 hours looking at a PC, and how was yours?"

"I phoned them."

"Who?"

"The doggers."

"What?!!!

"The people with the puppies for sale."

"Oh, wondered what you meant! Really? You didn't?"

"Yep, we have an appointment to see them on Thursday."

"OMFG!"

"Yes, OMFG!"

HEINZ 57

"Remind me what they actually are." my wife asked as I navigated around the lesser known streets of our city.

"Well it's a cross of a cross. Officially they're called Sprockerpoos."

"Eh?"

"I think it's a Springer Spaniel with a Cockapoo, which itself is a Cocker Spaniel with a Poodle."

"A mongrel."

"Don't say that, Heinz 57 please!"

I diverted the conversation away from the cruel sobriquets our quarry was gaining and reminded my wife:

"Now don't forget this is just a first visit, we're not committing to anything. We need to make sure we do all the right research first. Remember the flat we bought? That was a disaster, so we don't want that happening again – agreed?"

"Yep, let's take it nice and easy."

We arrived at the house which was not an obvious puppy farm, no blacked out BMW in the drive – phew! We knocked on the door and instantly there was a lot of barking going on. Introducing ourselves, loudly, above the barking, the lady showed us in. On the right was a white-ish dog, a Cockapoo going absolutely mental against a baby gate, while two children tried to watch TV, and in the hallway was a brown and white Springer Spaniel running around like a nutjob.

"This is "Maisey", the mum and that's "Winston" the dad."

I did a double take.

"That's the dad?"

"Yes, he's quite determined – he jumped the gate and found Maisey when we were out one evening."

"He jumped and then jumped then?"

My joke fell on deaf ears, although Winston looked like he was enjoying the comedy, or was it just the people. He looked like the sort of dog that enjoyed everything, shagging being high up on the list. But at least he was white-ish and Maisey was brown and white and big – so surely if it worked out we'd have something that was not too big and not brown?

The dining room had been converted into a Pet's Corner with a massive fence holding back the puppies, while two Terrapins eyed everything from their tank – did I see a cat too? Oh well the puppies would be used to other humans and animals, that was an important factor, apparently.

The whole puppyfest looked like a military exercise with a whiteboard on the wall detailing all the things that were going on with each individual puppy. Weight, size, chipped, largest poo, first word spoken, longest wee, that kind of thing. There were nine puppies listed, the last one out sadly hadn't made it, "man down", well "dog down" and one of them was going to be kept as company for Maisey and Winston – or perhaps to act as either a referee or worse, a gooseberry if

59

Winston got his way again. Apparently he would not be getting his way as his pockets had been picked, which reminds me of a story about his namesake on a similar subject. At some social gathering Lady Astor noticed that Winston Churchill's flies were undone. Tactfully she told him, to which he replied "Dead birds don't fall out of nests." Poor old Winston, the dog, his "nesting days" were over too, as were his "vaulting over the gate" days – although he wouldn't have to jump quite so high now, what a star he was.

That left eight, but there were actually only three puppies available by the time we got there. Each puppy sported a different coloured collar and so the three remainers were pointed out to us – green, red and pink.

"Would you like to hold one?"

It was a bit of an "Is the Pope a Catholic?" type moment, and I was quickly given "Green" a boy.

OMFG!

Want.

Want.

Want.

Want.

Want.

The years of research, that we promised each other we would do, went out of the window. Green on go! He was so sweet, a bit sleepy; was there something wrong with him? Quick phone my daughter! No, he was just tired as all his siblings seemed to be. I held him up in a bit of a Lion King moment and knew straight away he was the one. He was beautiful even though he was nearly all brown, except for a white goatee beard, very cool, and a white blaze down his chest. So, so cute – we both melted – he looked like a chocolate brownie, almost good enough to eat. My wife looked as if she had run her own "WantApp" and fortunately she agreed about Green, well almost, there was a bit of negotiating (whether we should take all three) and very quickly we were the proud owners, parents (!), of an almost 8 week old Sprockerpoo, and significantly poorer than when we arrived. Reader we just bought him!

"What have we done?"

"We've just gone and bought a dog, that's what we've done."

"Blinking flip" I didn't say.

THAT'S THE GAME OF THE NAME

There was a stunned silence as we drove home, each mile increasing the absurdity of what we had done. Let's recap:

Message from daughter with a link to puppies for sale.

Check out the breeder with "Mastermind".

See the puppies.

Buy one that is not likely to be small and is brown.

As somebody said to my wife later, "Well you weren't going to go and see them and not buy one were you?"

All that research! To be honest, there was something slightly distasteful in pitching up to a suburban house, meeting two strangers, and parting with a large sum of money for a live animal. To this day I am not sure how I feel about it, it is odd, but hey-ho, far be it from me to complain. It would be rather hypocritical too.

Beers and wine were served and quickly we were soon messaging our kids:

"New addition to the family!!"

"Seriously?"

"Yes we have, really! Gorgeous little puppies, we chose a boy, so sweet, should be ready in 2 weeks! You need to think of a name as well."

Many years ago I read a book called "The Running Sky" by Tim Dee. It was fundamentally about bird watching but he also tried to tie in literature with an avian theme. I found it dull and said so in an

Amazon review. One of the bits that really irked me was when Tim goes off to see a Starling roost with millions of birds. When he gets back he writes down 35 things that remind him of Starlings, four pages worth, from Bertolt Brecht to Laurence Sterne to Coleridge to Yeats and John Clare (whom he is obsessed with).

But now I am going to be mega-hypocritical. When it came to choosing the "all important" name, I don't think I have ever been involved in a more irritatingly long and stupid process, and believe me it's up against some stiff competition compared to the world of regulated medical devices! The message "You need to think of a name as well" precipitated a deluge of suggestions. My rule was that it must NOT be a human name, so "Nicky" was not allowed but "Waggy" was. But of course that was ruled out because, well because simply nobody could replace Waggy.

So Tim Dee, I apologise right here and now.......

Charlie.

Duder.

Daniel.

I mean FFS, Daniel, Daniel the bloody Spaniel – no, no, no, no, no!

Chastoo.

This was an abbreviation of Charlie Two. Charlie was one of our guinea pigs and my muse when I was "out of sorts", code for unemployed, years ago. One day Charlie shat the biggest guinea pig poo known to mankind. I Googled this, knowing it probably wasn't good news. It wasn't, he snuffed it a few days later, I was heartbroken. Charlie was never going to be the right name!

Reginald or Reg.

Mutley.

Archie.

I sent a message:

"Mum says Archie, please join me in saying that's shite"

"That's wanky"

"She wanted Archie for Todd"

"Let it go Mum"

Wilson.

Dullard.

Smew.

Gaston.

Vanker.

Sprue.

Tonka.

My wife is French so there was from time to time a Gallic theme....

Connard.

Uncle Toi.

Napoleon.

Napster.

Not-Todd.

Nobby.

Penis.

Bellend.

Ballsac.

Pube.

Scrotum – Word Association Football (Monty Python sketch) had taken over!

Gooch.

My reply was:

"Gooch is good"

"Please tell me you know what a Gooch is…" my daughter messaged.

"I thought you meant Graham Gooch the cricketer?"

"I've just informed Dad of what the word gooch means" my son posted.

Gooch got canned immediately, good though it was…..

Pedro.

Starsky. (I am surprised Hutch was not next, kids are too young I guess).

Pi.

Sheldon.

Snoop Dawg.

Dawgster.

Ghandi.

Floyd.

Mont St Michel.

Tintin.

Pluto.

"Pluto and Tintin are good"

"Pluto is rubbish, you'll look like Disney obsessives" our son could be so brutal.

Fergal.

Sharkey (sorry made that up for Word Association Football reasons).

San Miguel.

Goofy.

Mufasa.

Muttfasa.

Milo.

Chocky.

Chase.

Cucumber.

Chox.

Chox struck me as a good name, "Chox away" appealed to my love of aviation. I was pressing for this to be the one. But sadly it was rejected and the names kept streaming in. My sister got in on the act with the pathetic Bimber, Fairfax, and Walnut although Haggis got a few votes as did the next one.

Peanut.

Were we getting near? Scrolling through my phone as I write this, it doesn't look that way! Peanut was quickly dismissed because it fell into the same category as "Cucumber" my son said, which was code for "that's crap".

The next message was a picture of a bottle of wine my daughter had opened – tired or bored or both?!

Chien, so back to French….

Zoot – Zoot had been a favourite from previous discussions at Christmas, the "Dogless, mean Christmases" I'd like to remind you of, that I had experienced. But apparently, phonetically, it had other connotations….

Then came "Chocky" slightly based on Chox. My immediate thought was that Chocky was a book by John Wyndham, as in "The Day of the Triffids", that I had read about 40 years before. The plot is basically about a boy who has an imaginary friend who turns out to be an alien consciousness communicating with the boy's mind. I really did not want the dog to be some sort of psycho and was worried that shouting out "Chocky" might be a bit too much. My son summed it up succinctly:

"No it's a shit name anyway."

Monty (he might dig for freedom with that name).

Mooty.

My wife and daughter liked Mooty,

"It's weird but I quite like it." she messaged.

67

"Mooty is terrible" came the young voice of reason.

Twix.

Monkey.

Merlot.

Merlin.

Poldark, strangely "Antiques Roadshow" didn't appear.

Benson.

Bilbo.

Ralph.

Rolo.

Pongo.

We received a bumper crop from my daughter:

Captain.

Bart.

Bark.

Scilly.

Bentley.

Toad.

Frog.

Barney.

My response was

"Bentley is good, but is still a human name. The rest are shit."

Filou.

Sweepie.

Sweep.

Bounty.

Vino.

Mars.

Bear.

Scout.

Remi.

My son had recently moved into new accommodation at university and so there was a message from my wife:

"How was your first night in your new pad?"

I thought that was the best name suggestion so far that day.

We were sitting on the sofa, boring ourselves stupid with the "Word Association Football Name Game", when suddenly my wife said "How about Banxie?". Normally my Pavlovian response would be "No that's rubbish." but it struck me dumb. What a great name – I liked it!!! I "ran it up the flag pole and saluted it" in true management speak. Shocked by my reaction she immediately said "No, it's no good" – but it was too late. Chox got chucked and we banked Banxie (b'dum tschhhh!).

We test drove the name to a few people and there was general agreement, except from our son.

"That's shite."

So Banxie it was.

PART 3

PUPPY INCOMING

The next day I woke up, in fact we woke up, and realised what we had done. It was a mixture of a "new dawn" in our lives and possibly a "new nightmare" too. Between us we had racked up perhaps 2 days' worth of dog-sitting, hardly preparation for taking on a puppy.

We had "ummed" and "hahhhed" about getting a rescue dog, and in fact came close to owning one when "Mabel", a little Heinz 57, became available. But my wife only saw the "Mabel needs a forever home" message after Mabel had been nabbed by someone else. I really wanted a puppy, for no reason other than they are so cute – I didn't think anything else but that. That was a massively dumb mistake!

For the next few days my wife Glugled – Glued To Google - performing the research we should have done, talk about horse, bolted and stable. Still at least it was a dog and not a horse. Lists were drawn up, trips to "Dogs and Spencer" as I called it, even more money disappearing from our accounts and eventually we had everything we thought we might need. In retrospect we probably had 20%! All seemed fine as we finally agreed on the date to pick him up. Our daughter who happened to be back with us for a weekend volunteered to go and check him out for us, but we declined.

"But what if he's got an under- or overbite, a cleft palate, heart murmur, hernias, only one testicle, dodgy heart or dodgy lungs?" she said, trying to, and succeeding in, making us feel guilty as sin.

"He'll be fine, he looks normal, one heart and two of everything else."

"Only two legs then?"

"Yes, two at the front and two at the back."

It was uncomfortable having your own Vet to hand. All we had done with him was to pick him up and say "Awwww." We could have looked at the bite and palate I guess, cuddled him, hernia check perhaps, and then put him back in the cage but where was the fun in that? I had no idea if he had any testicles let alone two. Mine were missing after my daughter's questions; he was moving, so we could at least assume his heart and lungs worked to some extent. In truth it was pretty poor really, we should have checked things out much better, but, well I have no excuse, we just didn't, we were puppy morons really! I just hoped we hadn't missed anything obvious, "my goodness he's got no nose, how will he smell?" and that all his medical records were real and up to date. Hope "Springers" eternal. Yikes!

The big day dawned and I must admit I woke up and felt hugely apprehensive. Not particularly for the welfare and upbringing of the puppy, more for the fact that my mind was telling me that this day, this sunny Autumnal Friday was the end of my, well not to be selfish, our, freedom.

This evening everything would change. When our daughter was born (our first child) we naively said that we would not let the arrival of a baby change anything. We would carry on as normal. I mean how stupid was it to think like that? That lasted a few seconds and then for the next 25 years or so (with our son born a few years after) our lives were completely transformed, but for the good of course!

With our daughter working and our son at Uni we had had an extended period of *"sans enfants"* and, as I didn't work, I had had a short period of *"sans travail"* which was pretty good if not a bit boring. Well that boredom was going to be removed swiftly. Neither of us made the comment "We won't let the arrival of a puppy change anything", in fact it was more like "WTF are we going to do now?"

It nudged towards 6pm and I heard the car draw up.

"Ready?"

"Yep."

"Let's do this thing."

I really can't say if I was excited or not. Apprehension remained. No, let me be honest, I was shitting myself. It was that feeling of "it's too late, what on earth have we done?" feeling. It also seemed bizarre that in a few minutes we'd be returning "+1", that "+1" being a little puppy called Banxie – weird!

We arrived and were greeted by the cacophony of barking dogs, mainly Maisey and bollockless Winston and then were shown into the makeshift petting zoo at the back of the house.

"Oh goodness, you've grown!"

Seemingly Banxie and his siblings had grown 50% bigger since we first saw them – who'd have thought it?! They looked huge in comparison to our first encounter. There was some paperwork to sort out, which didn't take long and then there was a bit of an awkward moment with the breeders when I said I'd pay the balance when I got back, I think they smelt a dog robbery. But fortunately, unusually perhaps, French diplomacy came into play and we managed to transfer the funds (it really is a bit tacky) and all was happy. We picked up "Greeny", he still had the collar on, and walked to the car.

We both felt so guilty taking this little fella away from his siblings and his Mum, so cruel. But it was too late, we were in the car and off home, "+1".

PART 4

HOMEWARD BOUND

The journey was no more than 10 minutes, and Banxie sat on my wife's lap not doing much. Probably confused as to what was going on, no siblings, no mum, worse, no food!

I had imagined arriving and putting him down on the hall floor and him sitting and whimpering, looking at us for help and support. I was badly mistaken. Any worries we may have had about him being upset seemed unfounded as he appeared to not give a shit about his family and confidently started wandering around the house. That was a bit of a relief to be honest, at least he wasn't going to be a whinger, we hoped.

Very shortly he was definitely at home, peeing on the kitchen floor. Sadly the strategically placed puppy floor nappy thing remained unsoiled. We moved it to where he had peed and hoped for the best, only for him to piss where it had been!

I cracked open a beer, as you do on a Friday night, well every night to be honest, and sat down to watch the "entertainment show". Banxie was certainly inquisitive, poking his nose into anything and everything he could find, his little tail wagging incessantly. With the kitchen ticked off he then decided to give the hall a go. As halls tend to be, this was pretty dull, although he definitely noted that a slate floor would be a great place to drop some bodily fluid. Hall done, it was off to the lounge. Our beautiful lounge with the lovely walnut floor. Off he scampered around the room, and around and around, sniffing, crouching, sniffing, crouching, it seemed as if his batteries were running out, sniffing, crouching and then, arching. And. Then. It. Happened. Right before my eyes, this little puppy throttled a king-size Mars bar onto the floor. At first I thought he had some chameleon like qualities, it was well disguised against the wood floor, but this was quickly forgotten as my olfactory organs got to work. OMG. What a stink, I was waiting for the nuclear alert to sound. Wah, wah, wah, wah, wah, wah, wah, wah. What to do? Er, um, er, um and then it happened again. I lost my "turd-picking-up" virginity. Breathe through your MOUTH, black bag out, unfurl black bag, hand inside, crouch, pick, warm sensation, try not to gag (too much), rotate bag, inspect floor to make sure you have got it all, inspect bag (because we all look at poos don't we?) and then cleverly tie it off, with about 20 knots. I am not sure to this day why I tie so many, it doesn't make any difference, just feels like it does.

I DID IT! I FUCKING DID IT! I PICKED UP A DOG TURD, DIDN'T GAG AND MANAGED TO GET IT INTO THE BAG WITHOUT A FUSS - RESULT!

Banxie wandered off, lighter, and happier, but at least he didn't step in it, nor did I, well not that time. We tried to bring a bit of normality to proceedings and decided to sit in the lounge and see what he would do. He was happy enough to run around investigating and as he got more and more tired I picked him up and sat him on my lap, and we watched TV together until he fell asleep, bless. One thing I noticed, was the weird way he lay, front legs facing rearwards, like some amphibian - was he a fake dog and was in fact going to metamorphosise into a gigantic newt later on?

"Time for bed" said Zebedee (again for the older readers amongst you) and it was time to test out the bed. My wife had bought tons of stuff for Banxie's arrival (alcohol and crisps mainly) which included bedding that would fit inside a "crate". I think crates are a reasonably new idea, certainly in my early dog years of experience I never saw them. Our neighbours had a dog and one of the first things I remember him telling me was how fantastic their dog was:

"Oh she is the best at puppy class, she got a gold star you know."

"Oh how simply wonderful." I lied.

I mean FFS, fancy bragging about your bloody dog! (Hmmm, read on!) The neighbour did offer some advice, which was useful and that was "get a crate". I guessed he didn't mean beer (shame) and further assumed it was spelt "C-R-A-T-E" and not "K-R-A-I-T" which would have been a whole new world of entertainment with a dog, or even just the krait on its own (it's a snake). Very kindly BSJ donated his crate to the cause, and gingerly we picked up Banxie and took him to his bed for the night.

I can see it as a Disney film, a little puppy all dewy eyed with a big tear running down its cheek being placed into this massive crate. Let's be honest "crate" would be the term for inhabitants of Knightsbridge, you know the people who think "sex" is what you have your coal delivered in and a "creche" is a collision between two vehicles - just like our neighbours. It was a big black prison, not a crate, and we were putting this little mite inside, we felt awful.

"Night, night, back soon." I lied.

A true Oscar winning performance ensued, but we decided we would be tough. He would sleep in the crate, in the kitchen, end of. We did the walk of shame up the stairs and waited. And waited. And waited. Nothing. Was he dead? Back down to the kitchen, no he's fine. Back to the bedroom. Repeat a few times. Okay leave it. A bit pissed, I fell asleep and was suddenly violently awoken by a whimper. "Sssssssshhhhh" (you little bastard) we chorused and off we both went to the land of nod.

"Oh my God, it's eight o'clock, what about Banxie?!"

I suppose it could have been worse, at least I remember we now had a dog. Like a massive wave rolling over us, guilt appeared. Neither of us wanted to be the first to discover what had happened in the kitchen. The silence was deafening. We got up and ran down the stairs expecting the worse. Banxie's expression was as if to say:

"I have my breakfast at 7:30am, what kept you?"

Aw, the little bundle of joy was alive and champing at the bit to get out of his cage. Door open, out he trotted and pissed on the floor, away from the nappy of course, but the look of concentration on his face as he did it was funny. He really was a handsome little boy, lovely colour and such soft fur. Obviously he had "Spaniel ears" so pretty big and

79

these ears were very much a feature of his facial expression. Ears raised, head cocked to one side and he was listening (this did not happen very often as he was always way too busy for that), ears down "I am in trouble", or "I am scared" or "I just did something that I know I shouldn't have but hopefully you won't find it". He was impossibly cute! As well as the ears up and down, Banxie had two other facial manoeuvres that happened on a regular basis. One was when he moved in a way that folded one of his ears back, revealing the pinky inside. He looked ridiculous. Sometimes when he ran, both ears folded back, double ridiculous. But my favourite was when his gums folded in on themselves. Normally only one side at a time, but sometimes, both sides. It looked as if he was really perplexed about something, or really thinking hard about some issue of the day. Very funny too. I always say "Put your teeth back in Banxie", but of course he has no clue what that means, but knows it is a command. So then we have the cuteness of his ears up and him looking a bit perplexed - bless he is such a sweetie.

Breakfast done, we took him outside to try and inspire him to do a poo there, nice scenery etc. He wasn't having any of this, feigning anxiety he rushed back into the kitchen and laid a massive cable, off nappy, of course. My second "bagging" within 24 hours, I was getting to be an expert but was astonished that such a small dog could produce such large poos. It looked as if he had emptied his entire digestive tract. Interesting colour, more of which later.

Back outside and he had the decking to contend with. This in itself wasn't an issue, but there were some steps to negotiate. This didn't go well. Firstly he ran around trying to work out what these things were, and then sadly, he found out that steps can bite as he tumbled down them onto the grass. He looked around "Did I look cool?". No Banxie, but you did look sweet. Having fallen onto the grass his next mission was to get back onto the decking. The first step wasn't a problem, he managed that one, but the second higher one he just couldn't do. A helping hand assisted his ascent and all was hunky dory for a few seconds as the entire performance repeated itself. What could be better on a Saturday morning than to watch a tumbling puppy. Heart-warming stuff indeed.

For the rest of the day it was a continuation of entertaining him. If you thought it was hard with children, wait till you have a puppy. "Do you want to watch Peppa Pig?" simply isn't going to work. Food and drink does, (that was just for us), although apparently (the book said) not all dogs are food motivated? Who were they trying to kid? The only dog I can think of that wouldn't be food motivated would be a dead one or one without a mouth! Banxie was definitely food oriented, he never missed an opportunity if there was something to eat on offer.

And so began the routine. Wake up, breakfast, try and entertain him, lunch, try and entertain him, my wife arrives home, dinner, (beer and crisps, and that was just Banxie) try and entertain him, bed time. All this spattered, literally, with wee and poo breaks. Mind you he was pretty easy to entertain, everything was of interest inside or outside the house, good and bad, so all we had to do was just make sure he didn't get into trouble. You may wonder why I included the advent of my wife arriving home. This is because in Banxie's world it was a momentous event. He would hear her car draw up and park, and this would mean he was off to the gate (essential) by the kitchen door. Paws up on the railings, trying to look through them, tail going 19 to the dozen. In she would come

"Hellllloooo Bankzy, how are you?"

He made these lovely little whimpers and his whole body shook, rattled and rolled. When he rolled he peed everywhere, but it did have one advantage, you could put your foot on his tummy and move him around the kitchen floor like a mop to clean it up. I never imagined that was something a puppy could do. I jest, but you could move him around like a mop, he loved that!

This might sound simple. It should be really, but I was amazed how easy it was to lose him. One minute he would be there, the next we were calling him, fretting that he had dived in the pond, or worse, escaped. Then there was the worry that he would eat something he shouldn't. Right from the off he had a fascination with wood. Two massive oak trees in the garden in Autumn were manna from heaven for him as countless twigs, branches and bloody acorns fell all around him - he was spoilt for choice! Back then he was so tiny that it was relatively easy to remove the offending object, although this was only ever temporary, the next offending object was not far away.

AH, MIGHT AS WELL JUMP (JUMP)

I guess I wasn't entirely sure, or perhaps I was just delusional, about how he would "work" when we got him. I assumed he would be a bit like a computer, a sort of "plug and play" - we'd get him home and automatically he would work and that would be it, a super-duper Tamagotchi. I don't think I ever realised the true gravity of the situation when it came to training, I thought he would just be trained.

Someone once said:

"Labradors come into this world half trained and Spaniels leave this world half trained"

I really hoped this would not be true.

We did try quite hard with some basic stuff (more of which later) and he just about managed to "sit" when commanded (of course, only because there was food). It did seem that he responded to his name "Bank....Syyyyyy", but in truth he responded to any two syllables or even noises, but he really did seem to understand "Let's go back inside", but I expect that was because I was motioning to move there anyway - or was he really smart?! But anyway, I just could not get it out of my head that he didn't understand English. My wife is French, he didn't understand her either, mind you, who understands the French?!

The one thing he was incapable of understanding was "Don't". My real memory of this relates to jumping. I was reminded of that magnificent comedy series Fawlty Towers and in particular the very first episode called "A Touch of Class". Basil tries to improve the class

84

of the clientele but gets duped by a conman calling himself Lord Melbury. The Lord asks Fawlty to look after a briefcase which apparently contains expensive jewellery. When it is revealed that Melbury is a fake, Sybil decides to open the briefcase to see what is inside - the conversation goes like this:

Sybil: "Lets have a look at those valuables"

Basil: "What are you doing Sybil?.....Sybil, I forbid you to open the safe (she opens the safe) Sybil I forbid you to take that case out (she takes the case out) Sybil do not open the case I forbid it (she opens the case - to find bricks as it happens).

And this is what it was like with Banxie. It started when he put his paws up on the settee because he was too small to jump up. I picked him up. My wife came into the room and he stood up, tail wagging (as ever) and appeared to be getting ready to jump off. I was really worried as it was quite high and I thought he might injure himself.

"Banxie, what are you doing? I forbid you to jump!" he jumped.

Not long after that we were in bed and he was allowed upstairs - which is code for he managed to escape upstairs the little git. Actually while we are on the subject of stairs, his first attempts at an ascent were reminiscent of Monty the burrowing hamster, big stretch pull up and, depending on his luck, up to the next step, or remaining where he was. If he wasn't on the ground he might even go back down one or two - it really was one of those awful slow progress models in life, one stair up, two back down. Eventually though, he mastered it, and this was pretty early on, within a few days, he was so determined.

85

Anyway back to the bed. My wife, I'll blame her again, went to the bathroom. Dogs don't miss anything, even when they are sleeping, and straight away he was up wondering what was going on. The bed was significantly higher than the settee and I thought no way will he attempt to jump.

I could see him sizing it up and just said:

"Banxie, I forb...!" he jumped, again.

And when he jumped it was not a sort of "legs stretched out" to minimise the distance he had to leap, it was like a "Thelwell" pony cartoon with front legs pointing horizontally forwards and rear legs the mirror image of the front. Off he flew and crashed and burnt. Well he didn't burn but instead ran round to my side of the bed and placed his paws up on the bed begging to get back on it.

"Okay, little man, up you come."

You can guess the rest - he just carried on jumping, he really didn't give a shit about any friendly human advice.

The daily routine generally carried on as normal. I was very reluctant to leave him on his own (on reflection this was a big mistake, should've been harder on him) but from time to time I did. Not for long, except when I had to pick my son up from university and got stuck in traffic. Five long hours later I imagined the worst, dead dog, poo, piss everywhere, terrible smell etc., etc - but there he was in his cage wagging his tail, with a bladder the size of a football. He looked at me as if to say "Where have you been? I need to piss like a racehorse".

Most weekdays my wife would get up and sort him out and then bring him upstairs when she left for work. After trying to entertain him for an hour (meaning trying to get him to sleep) and failing, I would get up and make a tea and go into the garden. Then, tut, tut, I would spill a bit of tea onto the decking so he could lick it up - which he loved. I was told that teabags were biodegradable so as I like my tea very strong the teabag would still be in the mug when I went outside. Once, I threw the teabag away in some dense foliage. A minute or two later emerged a dog with a tea leaved face.

"Oh Jesus Christ, Banxie come here." he didn't, the tea bag was much too much fun, so was giving me the run-around.

Twice a week I would do a short 15-20 minute run. I hated running when I was at school, I hated running when we first had Banxie and even though I don't do it anymore, I hate it. I would shut him in his crate, say "Back soon" and off I would go for a bit of cardiovascular exercise - it was awful, although I did once manage to run 30 minutes non-stop which wasn't bad. When I got back he would be waiting for me, not because he was pleased to see me but because when we went outside for the morning tea he had the added bonus of licking all the salt off my legs from the sweat! Yuk! He's the only one that's disappointed that I don't run anymore.

After slurping tea off the decking and licking my legs Banxie would need some "love".....if I sat on the decking he would come up to me and basically walk onto my lap looking for a cuddle. This was very sweet except he always wanted to lick my face. This is something really not sweet, in fact it's more likely to be bitter, as he had probably just licked his willy or similar - eurgh! And, irrespective of what the last thing he had licked was, it just made my flesh creep, still does to this day - it's almost as if it's two magnets in opposition such is the repulsion.

Unsurprisingly he needed almost constant attention, and as I said before you can't just plonk him in a puppy chair and give him some toys, or stick on a DVD. A typical session in the garden was, Janet and John style:

"See Banxie run, oh look at him go, the little puppy." (sweetness 1.0)

"See Banxie dig a fucking great hole in the lovely lawn." (incandescent 1.0)

"Don't see Banxie, panic, has naughty Banxie escaped?" (heart attack 1.0)

"See Banxie almost fall in the pond." (heart attack 2.0)

"See Banxie drink the blanket weed infested water." (idiot dog 1.0)

"See Banxie eat pigeon poo." (idiot dog 2.0)

"Grab Banxie and tell him off." (miserable human 1.0)

REPEAT for as long as you can stand it. (So not very).

Initially it was all wonder and new, this little bundle of fur having a great time and the onlookers enjoying all the fun. But after a week or two, I am sorry to say, it did get on my tits a bit and so then we would go inside. I would feel guilty that I was so intolerant and so soon, we would return to the garden where the whole thing started over again. The poor little mite, it wasn't his fault. I spent a lot of time working out just how long it was until I could take him out into the big wide world, that day couldn't come quick enough. But I'll be brutally honest, sometimes it was boring, routines are though aren't they? Not always though, and some days were better than others. But there's only so much you can do with a young puppy that is confined to the house and garden. (Strictly speaking this isn't true, you can take them outside your house, but as they aren't vaccinated it is a bit like not having Avast (other anti-virus software is available) loaded up on your PC. Of course you could always buy an Appledog - no anti-virus required but expensive).

I found it difficult to understand that the modus operandi of dogs is basically the above, that's what they do all the time they are awake, apart from eating, and occasionally (though it appeared not to be in Banxie's case) resting. Quite why I hadn't figured that out beforehand is beyond me, perhaps I didn't want to consider it and just assumed it would "be fine" - bad research!

On the theme of "rest" in the afternoon, I would try and get him to be calm on the bed and hopefully have a little nap. I am not sure why, but there was an almost "Pavlovian" response to being on the bed. It wasn't a pleasant one. I could see him work it out - "On the bed therefore I must start..............biting." This is one thing that was not a constant over that first month. Initially he would just lick your fingers or have a bit of a nibble, his teeth little blunt stubs - it was, in a way, quite pleasant, soothing almost. But as time progressed his teeth got longer and much, much sharper, and anywhere on the body was fair game. Toes being bitten was agony - this I am sure would be worthy of torturing people to confess, just get a puppy in and let them bite their feet. Pushing him away was the worst thing you could do because that turned it into a game - and hiding in the bed only worked for a while, until he was big enough to jump up onto it to attack.

It got so bad that in the morning when my wife brought him upstairs, or he made it on his own, I had to hide under the duvet as he tramped all around biting me through the covers. When I appeared, my bald head was the target for nasty nibbling and as more of my head appeared so the target increased in size. It was agony, needle like tattooing (I don't have a tattoo so I am guessing here) followed by licking followed by more needlework. By this time I would need a call of nature so would get out of bed, on the wrong side (literally and metaphorically) and make for the loo - not quick enough, toes and ankles bitten - hideous.

WTAF did we get a dog for?!!!

But making it to the loo was a double edged sword. Banxie would follow me in, nipping at my heels, yet would stop as soon as I started to pee. Why? Because once I got out of the way a new, far more interesting goal appeared - bog roll. That Andrex dog has got a lot to answer for; but at least it gives you an idea of what will happen. Always, always mid-stream and he was off - paws against the wall, mouth open, teeth in and ruuuuuuuuuuuuuuuunnnnnnnnnnnnnnnnnnnnnn awayyyyyyyyyyyyyyyyyyyyyyy!

It was everywhere, and not in one piece. Oh no, that would be simple, no let's make a real game of it and chew it up, spit it out, hide under the bed and spit some more out etc. Mornings were such a joy! When I had de-bogrolled the bedroom, inspected my wounds to see if they spelt anything like "Mum" and "Dad" or "Love" and "Hate" or "You're a shit Human" it was time to progress downstairs..........well you know that routine now.

In the end it all got too much for me, pathetic I know. One afternoon I called my wife "You'll just have to come home early, I can't do this any more, Banxie is driving me nuts." It wasn't quite like that, every other word was probably "ahhh" or "owww" as Banxie, completely oblivious to what was being said, continued to tattoo any part of me he could sink his teeth into.

For the second time in a few months I was a broken man. I didn't blub this time, and in fact got a deserved bollocking from my wife for being pathetic. It was fair enough, I was being pathetic. All I was asked to do was look after a puppy all day - easy peasy. Well let's just see how you get on eh? Is there a Samaritans for dog owners? And on that point, I had read that one benefit of owning a dog is companionship which may help with stress and mental health. Without wishing to be facetious, all I could see was that Banxie was actually a detriment to my mental health! That is so unfair, sorry. Poor little thing. He sat there with his ears up looking at me as if to say "I'm only a puppy, this is what puppies do." (tactfully leaving out "you pathetic Human") - how could I not care for him? So much.

He was cute, no doubt - so cute that at the end of the day I always forgave him, bless. Particularly as I sentenced him to a night in the crate - ah peace perfect peace. When he looked at me through the ~~prison bars~~ crate his little face did seem to forgive me too - or at least that's what I told myself. It was heartbreaking really.

We had to wait about a month from getting him (I think it was actually 783 hours, not that I was counting) until he was allowed out in the big wide world. The daily routine continued but there were a couple of other things that happened.

Firstly, I was quite surprised at the number of "friends" I didn't know we had who dropped by, not to see us but to see the "Ooooh you've got a new puppy". These visits were rather good actually, for three reasons: firstly it meant Banxie got a new toy to rip to shreds, secondly it meant that he was bothering other people for attention for a while, and thirdly and without doubt the most entertaining part was when he first saw the visitors. It was amusing to hear them squeal with delight at his cuteness and then to watch their faces drop as he performed a long "happy wee" - sometimes on himself, sometimes on the floor, but quite often over them - don't think he's so cute now do you eh?!

The other item on the agenda was "vaccination". Now then, until my relatively recent foray onto Twitter I never knew about the "Anti-Vaxx" movement - a group of ~~twats~~ people, in the conspiracy theory vein, who think that vaccines don't work. Quite how they think e.g. smallpox was dealt with is beyond me but there we go. So please get your animals vaccinated, don't believe any of that Anti-Vaxx shite, vaccines work.

I digress, sorry, but it was an important digression. Dogs get vaccinated to protect themselves, *and other dogs of course,* from some real nasty stuff such as distemper, hepatitis, parvovirus and leptospirosis, and for us there was no debate, we would get Banxie vaccinated. Vet visits in detail are coming up later, but something the Vet said to us rang a bell. I am sure my nose grew too.

"We advocate positive reinforcement when training puppies." he said, in a way that was not at all aggressive, just assertive, a sort of, "if I hear you are not positively reinforcing your puppy when training it, I will personally come round and kick the shit out of you."

"Oh yes of course." we chorused. The image of my brother-in-law, with a rolled up Daily Mail whacking seven bells out of Ben came to mind - gulp. My own shouting at Banxie when he didn't pee on the mat, or (admittedly it was the last time) when he took a massive dump in our en-suite shower. Hmm.

93

We got in the car.

"Positive reinforcement?"

"Shit."

"Oops."

"Shit."

"Well from now on."

"Of course."

When we got home, Banxie ran around, chewed his toys and other things he shouldn't have, pissed all over the floor, bit us and generally caused trouble - a normal evening I suppose.

"Oh Banxie, how wonderful, good boy!" Said two pairs of gritted teeth.

After the second jab, and another two week wait, it was over, the next day he would be going out into the big wide world, positively reinforced of course.

THE ROAD IS LONG, WITH MANY A LAMPPOST

So here we are. Banxie has got his MOT (Mongrel Outside Ticket) he is taxed, well he has been taxing shall we say, he's full of fuel, two careful owners, ready to go. Or is he?

I've no idea what happened but somewhere between visiting the Vet and right now, Banxie has got really worried about leads, harnesses and the car. Let's have a look, hmm, probably not difficult to work out. He would be thinking "There I was enjoying myself when I was strapped into some S+M gear, unceremoniously put in this noisy thing that moved, taken out and carried to a room where I was physically abused." Not difficult to work out why he was somewhat reluctant to let me put the harness on him.

We had tried the lead and harness out in the garden and he seemed okay with it, and we'd also taken him outside the house to try to get used to the traffic, carrying him rather than letting him walk as he potentially wasn't fully immune, and again he seemed okay. But now, with the big wide world looming large, he had stage fright in heaps. Actually a better word would be in oceans, oceans of pee, all over the kitchen floor. Goodness me, it was terrible, poor little thing. His tail was well between his legs and his back made a lovely normal distribution curve but sadly the only standard deviation he made was to run under the kitchen table.

No amount of cajoling would get him out until I got him a treat. Treats are tremendous currency for dogs, well that is if your dog is motivated by food of course. Eventually I prised him out from under the table and got the harness on, only getting a little bit splashed in the intervening time.

"Oh Banxie, come on we are going for a lovely walk today."

At that point I don't think Banxie saw me as Mr Motivator, more like the crooks in 101 Dalmatians. Eventually I got him to the car and strapped him in. Then the next problem occurred. Dribble. Great ropes of it coming from his mouth and sticking on the car seat. He looked so miserable! I thought to myself maybe he really was a fake dog, I just couldn't understand why he didn't want to go out for a walk. Unperturbed (a complete lie, I was very upset) I drove off, not far, to what became known to Banxie and me as "Patch No 1". As I drove I did a mental check which is as important as the pre-flight checks when flying an aeroplane, though mercifully shorter:

Poo bags - check.

Treats - check.

Towel - check (it was Autumn).

Toys - check.

Beer and crisps - joke.

Phew, I had not forgotten anything!

Let me digress a bit here and talk about bird watching for a bit. You may recall, dear reader, that I mentioned I was a keen birdwatcher. Well if you regularly visit somewhere doing this hobby you probably will call it your "patch". This particular location was by a river, with lots of trees and wide open green spaces (an ex-pitch and putt course that I had played on many times in my youth) - it was a wonderful place to start walking him I thought - lots of different things to experience, including humans and other dogs. I knew I would take him here often, so thought while walking him I would start a list of birds that I saw, hence "Patch No 1" was born.

We parked and I opened the back door, de-slobbered him and lifted him out. I was even more convinced he was a fake then, as he transformed into a cheerful little cheeky puppy all happy as Larry. What a git. People we met would never believe me if I told him the palaver to get him there.

And off we went for the walk.

I like Mathematics so was pleased to see a formula had been calculated for the amount of exercise the average puppy should have (bearing in mind that I really don't think anything vaguely Spaniel can be called average). Anyway it went like this:

Minutes of exercise per day = 2 x (5 x age in months)

For Banxie who was precisely 3 months, this was 30 minutes a day, in two 15 minute sessions (that's why there is a "2" on the RHS of the equation). That seemed fine except it made no mention of distance. Perhaps it just assumed that you would be walking for 15 minutes at a go. Well we did try, but I probably only managed about 100m - why? Because when you have a puppy, and one as cute and handsome as Banxie, and there's lots of people, you won't get far.

He was pretty good on the lead, very good for a first proper outing, but not so good on the "happy-wee" front. In fact not only did he do human size poos, he seemed to be able to hold in a massive amount of wee, enough to meet many hundreds of people.

And the people, I have to say, were absolutely lovely. Every single one of them commented on his lovely colour, his sweetness, his ears, his wagging tail and oh, his piss all over my shoes and trousers.

"Is he a boy or a girl?" Many asked.

"He's non-binary actually."

I really wanted to say this, but I just didn't have the nerve. As we made our way slowly, he went off piste a bit into some mud, so the later "Coo-ers" got the added bonus of dirt on their trousers. I got used to warning them "Don't let him jump up, he's got muddy paws" but again, hearteningly, nobody seemed to care. I was really taken aback by this, people are generally nice to dog-walkers I thought.

All too soon it was over, and his first walk had been a complete success. I was so pleased, so proud too. "Proud Parent Syndrome"! As for the journey home, well just read the journey out bit, a few paragraphs above, and you'll get the idea. That aspect would need to be worked on, once he was out of the car he was fine, but the before and after wasn't pleasant for him at all, poor little devil, nor me either!

PART 5

LONG MAY YOU RUN, LONG MAY YOU RUN

Banxie's world took a big step, literally, that day and every day subsequently. We were back to a routine, but a different one whereby a proper walk was added to the list of activities. I have thought long and hard about this, and have decided that it would be pretty dull if I just wrote about what we did each day - got up, biting, wee, breakfast, biting, tea in the garden, poo and a wee, biting, walk, another poo and several wees, biting, rest, biting, wee, dinner, biting, my wife comes home, biting, wee, biting, a bit more biting and then, maybe a tad more before, sleep, perfect sleep, perchance to dream, of biting.

Therefore, what I thought would be better than a diary of walking Banxie was to look at certain aspects of ~~dogging~~, dog owning. You may have noticed that I have alluded to this throughout what you've already read, when I have said "More of which later". (I hope you didn't skip any, shame on you if you did, took me ages to write all this). I hope you like this change (tough if you don't, go and make a tea and sit outside), and let's kick off with "Walking". I know, I know, I said I didn't want to bore you with the daily walk, but some of those walks I have to tell you about..........ah actually they can wait, let's talk about something that is massively important for the dog owner, poo!

SHIT HAPPENS!

Certainly does! Regularly. I'll be honest, I have really been looking forward to writing about this. Someone once said to me that when a group of men get together, no matter what they talk about, they always end up talking about poo. I agree, although I would add, with some of my friends it's the first thing we talk about! A guy called Charlie who used to work for me, tremendous bloke, used to send me texts or WhatsApp messages which simply said "EB". I would reply "Nice, same here." or "Excellent, not here yet." EB was code for "Empty Bowels" and as his father had said to him "Charlie, there is no finer feeling than empty bowels son" - I have to agree. And I am sure Banxie would too.

If you are reading this in 2021BC (before canine) rather than 2021AD (after dog) then you need to have a serious conversation with yourself. And that conversation, or perhaps an essay you must write in your mind, is

"Face to face with faeces, can you face it?"

You need to sit down and ask yourself, seriously, what do you think about poo? Does it revolt you to see it? Does it make you gag when you smell it? Obviously I am talking about your own poo here, but once you've answered those questions, then please substitute your own poo for that of a dog. Imagine, if you will, a dog on the lush sward of a cricket pitch arching its back and dropping a string of warm, steaming turds onto the ground. Imagine further the colour, the smell, the size, the shape, the texture - how do you feel? Revolted? Cool? Unsure? Let me tell you, if you are revolted, then a dog is not for you, because those warm, steaming, turds are going to have to be picked up. By. You. Yes. You. No. Escape.

It works like this - first try an avoid seeing your dog dumping because then you can claim ignorance and leave the poo in-situ - ha, ha! Secondly, train your dog to poo well off-piste. Thirdly train it to pick it up itself. Now, here is a massively important point. People have suggested that having a dog is either easier than raising kids or harder. At the moment I am unsure, I might go for harder but time will tell. However, there is one MAJOR difference between dogs and kids......

Do you remember those halcyon days when the kids became potty trained? Even better, do you remember when nappies became a thing of the past? Deep, deep, joy. Well with a dog, those days will NEVER appear. You will ALWAYS be picking up poo - so get used to it, and if you don't think you can or ever will be able to, then a dog is not for you, definitely not!

The first time I ever saw someone pick up a poo was when I was driving to work one morning. I thought "What a great citizen", not realising that it was now the law. I ran through my mind what that person had done and was just disgusted. Little did I know that I would be that person a few years later, I have quite surprised myself!

I mentioned before that picking up a poo was a bit of an art and there are some important things I need to point out. Firstly, don't skimp on the quality of the bag and make sure it is black. Don't be fooled by all those jazzy colours, your dog doesn't care but the passers-by will, as you can see the turds through them - awful. Secondly practise opening the bag. I am totally inexpert at this. So once Banxie has logged out, I spend about 5 minutes trying to undo the bag, I just cannot do it. Women always seem to have the knack!

Once you have safely captured the canine nuggets (or worse canine Mr Whippy, difficult to capture to be honest) then make sure you dispose of your bag responsibly. We have rules about Banxie's poos which I think are reasonable, some readers may disagree but here goes. If he poos well off piste then we will go and inspect it (you always have to do this, like you do with your own) and then cover it up. If he poos a bit off piste then we will have a bit of a discussion and either flick it away to a safer place or pick it up. If he poos on the path or very near it, then we always pick it up. It is disappointing and, to be honest, shameful that many dog owners don't give a shit about their pooch's shit. Quite often we have to step over poos on the path (areas around car parks are a shit storm) or see bags just left by the side - "We'll pick it up later." they said, as I look at it for the fifth day running. I'd rather they just left the poo than a non-biodegradable bag there. Then worst of all are the "Damien Hirst / Tracy Emin" dog owners, those irresponsible bastards who think it is a hoot, or perhaps an art installation, to throw their laden bags into the surrounding trees and bushes. Oh how hilarious. Absolutely disgusting - the offenders should be made to clear up all dog poo in the surrounding area with bare hands. And just to give you some idea about how bad dog poo really is - here is an extract from a paper entitled:

"Environmental Contamination by Dog's Faeces: A Public Health Problem?"

It was published here: International Journal of Environmental Research and Public Health. 2013 Jan; 10(1): 72–84 and starts off with:

Dogs and cats live in close contact with humans. In particular, dog numbers have increased in industrialised countries. The presence of dog faeces in urban settings due to the habit of dog owners of not removing dog faeces from the street may represent a problem for hygiene and public health. Dog faeces may contain several types of microorganisms potentially pathogenic for humans.

Bacteria that are pathogens for the intestinal tract and cause diarrhoea include Campylobacter, Salmonella, Yersinia and E. coli

That was just the beginning of the introduction, there was worse! So act responsibly, please.

Inspecting your dog poo is important, you need to become a bit of a copraphile, because you may see some nasties in there that could tell of something more serious. Banxie dropped a turd once which at the end had blood on it. Fortunately it was bright red so I guessed it emanated near the end of the dung chute rather than a deeper more potentially serious region. On the other hand it can act as a relief. As an example I give you the case of the chewed flip-flop. Banxie was let loose in the garden and decided he would steal a flip-flop on his way out. Moments later and the flip-flop has flopped big time, bits are strewn over the decking and lawn and I can see him continuing to bite it. I manage to get it off him, but clearly he has eaten some. Hopefully he will be okay and hey presto, next day, the throttled Mars bar contains lots of blue flip-flop in it, straight through, no problem!

And dog poo will become a subject of discussion. (Actually, perhaps we are just weird, didn't think of that). The points of the conversation are:

"Did he do one?"

"How big was it?"

"What colour was it?"

"What texture was it?"

And very quickly this conversation becomes a brief morning report:

"Yes, enormous (it always is), brown, formed."

This gets a massive tick, this is normal poo, well done Banxie! No poo, in the morning, is very rare, and if that happens I know there will be a mudslide of gargantuan proportions later on. Texture is sometimes a worry - I mentioned before about "Mr Whippy" type poos. They don't appear to be unusual and don't appear related to any illness, perhaps having the shits is just normal, like humans, although be aware that if your dog runs around a lot he might have a Mr Whippy dump that I believe is related to adrenaline - all seems normal!

105

If you got a dog in 2020, or were researching one, then you will have come across new vocabulary such as "Lockdown", "Social Distancing", "Furloughed" and the more exotic "Anal Glands". My daughter first alerted me to these as she frequently mentioned that she was "sorting them out" with some of her clients. Dogs (and cats) have two small grape sized anal sacs near their bum hole. Their purpose is to release a few drops of scent marking fluid when your pet poos. Sometimes though they don't work so well, unfortunately for the animal, and, worse, unfortunately for you! Did you ever watch "You've been Framed"? There is a famous clip on there of a Shepherd singing a hymn by a five-barred gate with his adoring Border Collie looking on. Part way through the clip, the dog propels himself forward using only his front legs while wiping his arse all along the grass. Apparently, I have just found out, this is called "Scooting". And it is not confined to fields with Shepherds in them. Oh no, more often that not you will see your dog wiping its arse on your lovely shag-pile carpet or on the kitchen floor. Get the anti-bacterial spray out immediately! Further evidence is available if you see your dog eating grass. This may be simply a way of adding roughage to their diet, helping to keep them pooing regularly but it can mean other things, one of which is sub-optimal operation of the anal glands. Okay, you need to take a deep breath before you read this next bit, even if you are fascinated by poo, this takes some doing................

When the anal glands aren't working too well, and there is a lot of scooting and grass eating going on, be prepared. I wasn't, but fortunately quickly realised what was happening. We were out walking and Banxie did his usual circle turning, running, circle turning, I knew a poo was imminent. He got into position and strained and strained. Eventually some poo came out but.........it was a string of faeces encrusted grass....................which he just could not crimp off. What to do? He got really upset about this, and started trying to bite it off (OMG!). Had it been a little longer I could have trod on it, but it was just too short. So, black bag in hand, or over hand I should say, I bent down and pulled it out. He was really unhappy about this, trying to bite me, a bloody dangerous activity, biting near a swinging dog poo, but all was sorted in the end, from his end. I think he was grateful! This has happened twice in a year, so it is not that frequent, but from my daughter's probing we know his anal sacs could work better - and God do I wish they would!

I always assumed dogs were dirty creatures, pooing and peeing anywhere and everywhere, but this is not true. Once Banxie had received his MOT and Tax we found that he was actually quite reluctant to poo or even pee in the garden. Strangely, you might think, I actually preferred him to poo in the garden as he generally did it in muddy covered areas away from the lawn. However for a pee it was totally different. One day I looked out at the garden and wondered why it had become what looked like a practice area for carpet bombing, the green lawn littered with yellow dead areas. A vision of a squatting dog came to mind, and suddenly it all fell into place - I too was glad when he decided not to wee in the garden any more, but it was too late by then.

And something I have found curious, from a human point of view. When he poos he doesn't automatically have a wee at the same time, or just slightly afterwards - unlike humans. He might have a wee then a poo, or the reverse but never together. I discussed this with friends, who agreed this was weird compared with humans. Then I did a bit of Citizen Science. I went for a cable laying session in the inner sanctum and tried not to pee after the act. To my amazement it is possible! Not particularly comfortable, but definitely possible. Goodness me, the things you learn when you have a puppy!

Banxie must have some Camel genes in him somewhere. At first, worrier that I am, I thought he might be seriously ill as he didn't seem to drink much, but then I would catch him taking on what seemed like gallons of the stuff. And he has this incredible capacity to hold it all in, far better than me in my dotage. He can go for 12 hours or more without needing a wee or a poo. Actually he probably does need to go, what I mean is he can hold it in until it's okay to let it all go. I expected him to just go when he felt like it, but no, he is a very good dog in that respect and it is quite amusing to see the relief in his face when he has a sniff and cocks his leg - he's moved on from squatting as he has grown up.

A cautionary tale. I guess it had to happen, but I was surprised and bitterly disappointed when it did. It was in the early days of the big wide world experience and we were merrily making our way along the towpath of Patch No 1. Banxie was on the lead when he suddenly started turning circles, retracing his steps, turning circles. No need to panic, he is going to lay a cable I thought. Which he did. Normal. Bag out, breathe through mouth, fiddle to get it open, struggle to get to the pile because Banxie is pulling on the lead, bend down pick up, rotate to tie it off and, fuck no, oh no, it's on my hands. OMG what could I do? It is bloody difficult doing everything one-handed, yet I managed somehow and then decided to surreptitiously drop my hand in the river, hoping that nobody worked out what was going on. While the river removed some poo it didn't remove it all and I don't recall I had a tissue. I think I wiped my hand in some grass and continued on. Except that you can't. It's just like when you are a kid and hurt your finger and your whole arm becomes redundant. I walked back to the car, I do wonder if some people thought I had had a stroke, and managed to get him and myself inside, one-handed. I then drove home, also one handed, or steering with my wrists until salvation arrived in the form of some hot water and soap. Lesson learnt - take some bacterial wipes with you, you'll need them sooner or later, or get used to the taste of poo!

I've mentioned Banxie's bladder contents, and need to caution you again, well if you are a bloke rather than a woman - this isn't sexist this is practical. While out walking with him, out in the Forest rather than the very public Patch No 1, I would always need to answer a call of nature. For chaps this is easy, sorry ladies, that's "The Way It Is" as Bruce Hornsby said. But when I stopped to wee, Banxie, when he was young, would find this hugely entertaining and try to drink my wee, forcing me to keep on moving, something you really don't want to do mid-stream. You can imagine the result. So if your dog goes missing while you are having a wee, look downwards.

At my daughter's in darkest Wales at night I took him outside for a wee. The thought inspired me and, so I thought, we were in concert, him happily cocked over there and me here. I couldn't see him, it really was pitch black, but then I could see a form beneath me and realised I had pissed on the poor little fellow's head. It was pretty wet (it was November) so I just brushed a bit of rain water on his head and went back inside.

"It smells of dog wee in here." said my wife (she would beat a dog in a detecting smells competition).

"No it doesn't, it must be you." I replied.

"Yes it does a bit." said my daughter unhelpfully.

"No, it doesn't." my nose grew.

Confession is good for the soul, I was caught bang to rights - ooops - well at least Banxie got a nice head wash, some people pay good money for that. I was just sent to Coventry for the rest of the evening.

THE OTHER END

I think that is enough about poo don't you? There is of course another route out of the body, via the mouth. There is something comfortable about being in an EB situation but at the other end of the factory, it is a different story. Puking from a hangover rarely makes you feel better immediately, but I have puked from something I've eaten and felt better straight away, but not in an EB way. Dogs and cats seem to throw up fairly regularly with no ill effects, but of course if they are doing it all the time and there's nasties in it (e.g. blood) best get it checked out.

One thing I found odd, sorry we are returning to the other end briefly, but bear with, is that oddly, unlike other dogs and myself and most of my male friends, Banxie doesn't fart much. In the time we've had him I doubt he has, to my knowledge and nose, farted more than once a month. Very strange. Very welcome, dog farts are hideous. But one downside of this is it means I can't blame my over active bowel movements on him, shame. Where he really scores in the blokish slob stakes is belching. The test for a good belch is whether you can say "Kuala Lumpur" as it comes out. I am a master at this, give me a can of lemonade, and if I gulp it down I can produce a superb rendition of the Asian capital, and possibly the country and surrounding waters. Banxie's Geography knowledge is not great, but nevertheless, if he could articulate it, he would definitely be on his way to a KL one. They really are human burps, I have never seen that in a dog before. Unlike babies, who look surprised when they hear the sound, he is unfazed. He just lets it go and carries on - gets my vote, the slob.

Back to puking.

The first real puke Banxie did was fairly early on, one afternoon when my sister came to visit - I am sure the two were not related of course. We sat down to eat some "Lemon Drizzle Cake" she'd made, when I was distracted by a weird sound. Being a birdwatcher I couldn't help but think there was a Stock Dove in the kitchen, it certainly sounded as if there was one there.

"Wuuuumph, wuuuumph, wuuuumph, wuuuumph, wuuuumph, wuuuumph."

I looked down and saw poor little Banxie convulsing, clearly trying to get something out of him and then he produced it, a browny coloured pavement pizza. He looked startled by his own ability to produce something that seemed so large that it couldn't possibly have been concealed inside - but it had been - it was enormous. Banxie seemed to have the wrong size digestive tract plumbed into him. There he was a "Small" with what seemed like an "XL" GI system judging by the volume of excreta that emanated from him.

Relieved of this burden, Banxie perked up and ran around again wagging his tail.

"Wuuuumph, wuuuumph, wuuuumph, wuuuumph, wuuuumph, wuuuumph."

I looked down - uh oh. A side dish of pizza.

112

Not long after this......

"Wuuuumph, wuuuumph, wuuuumph, wuuuumph, wuuuumph, wuuuumph."

A pizza canape...

Not long after this......

"Wuuuumph, wuuuumph, wuuuumph, wuuuumph, wuuuumph, wuuuumph."

A pizza canape...

Not long after this......

"Wuuuumph, wuuuumph, wuuuumph, wuuuumph, wuuuumph, wuuuumph."

A pizza canape...

Not long after this......

"Wuuuumph, wuuuumph, wuuuumph, wuuuumph, wuuuumph, wuuuumph."

A pizza canape...

He just could not stop puking, it was everywhere. As fast as I cleared it up (not that fast in honesty, it was awful) he deposited another load. By this time he really did not look too clever and had voluntarily taken to his crate. I tried to get him out but he was not having any of that. His poor little face, Disneyesque, said "I am dying, please leave me alone." At one stage I thought he had died, he didn't move when I poked him, I admit I cried, the poor little mite.

I was really worried, this amount of puking, without the merest sniff of a beer, was not right, there was only one thing to do, call my daughter:

"Hi, it's Daddy."

"I know, what's up with Banxie now?"

"He's throwing up all over the place!"

"Take him to the Vet."

Five years of training, five years of sponsorship by the Bank of Mum and Dad and that was the best she could come up with FFS.

Banxie didn't make much of a fuss getting into the car and amongst the dribble, off we sped to see the Vet.

VET IT BE

Hands up if you like going to the see the Dentist, GP or going into hospital for an operation? That's very few of you and I am sure those of you with your hands up are not telling the whole truth. For me the Dentist isn't an issue, it very rarely hurts (particularly if you have good teeth) but even though I lie there telling myself it is "fine" I notice I tense up. I then tell myself to relax and all is fine for a few seconds until I realise I have tensed up again.

Imagine visiting any of the above but in a foreign country where you don't understand what is being said, and you're inside a cage not much bigger than yourself and you can only see out the front. I am guessing that must be what animals visiting the Vet must feel like, but probably a lot, lot worse. It must be awful for them. On the first visit it probably isn't so bad, it's all (horribly) new but soon they get wise to it. Todd the cat knows what's going on. If I pick him up, he looks me in the eye and I can see that he's saying "You never normally pick me up and be nice to me, I know where we're going, you bastard." Todd has never forgiven me for dropping him when my daughter brought the ginger whinger kitten home. It was a complete accident, he just jumped out of my hand. Crueller people have suggested I was checking out that he was a proper cat to make sure he landed the right way up - he did of course, but not very elegantly.

The Vet practice can be an interesting place for a human. Often very busy with lots of animals coming and going, mainly cats and dogs but the occasional exotic like an iguana or a goldfish (I mean who takes their goldfish to the Vet FFS?) and a whole spectrum of emotions on display by their owners. Apparently dogs take on the look of their owners - oh dear, poor Banxie, that lively little pup is going to end up as a fat, balding bastard. Poor thing.

Fortunately, (all bar one visit which I will tell you about later) prior to our visit today, the outcomes have been okay, so I am hoping that Lady Luck is smiling sweetly. Today was a rush so there wasn't time to get Banxie entombed, he's just "(ch)illing out" on the back seat of the car. As I open the back door I have another religious moment as the previously "on death's door" Banxie appears to have transformed into Lazarus. Here he is wagging his tail and jumping up at me - hmm.

I get inside, and to complete the experience, the Vet has a beard - oh. He looks Banxie over, and by now I am thinking that a bit of non-positive reinforcement might be in order - the little acting git. He is fine, I am no Vet but even I can see that. Just for good measure, perhaps it's to teach him a lesson, he sticks a thermometer up Banxie's arse, and in a homage to "Tom and Jerry" Banxie's eyes run down to the end of his front paws and shiver. (I am sure if animals just come in to have their nails clipped they still get a thermometer up the jacksy, it seems *de riguer* if you are a Vet). The Vet then consults a book, and for a moment I think he must be reading the Gospel of John (John 11:1–44) but in fact it is the "BSAVA Small Animal Formulary Part A: Canine and Feline" (so I have been reliably informed) from which he picks

116

some exotic potion and jabs it into Banxie.........as a precautionary measure.

"Be careful with his food, just bland stuff like boiled chicken and rice." he advises me.

Cuddles and stroking then take place (that's just me and the Vet) and off we go to pay.

Banxie is happy as Larry, I can't believe that not 30 minutes ago he was on death's door with a truly Oscar winning performance, yet here he is putting on the cuteness show to everyone as I watch my bank account get depleted. My older sister took Waggy to the Vet, I am not sure for what, something minor, probably he had shagged another fur coat and eaten some. Shocked at the cost of the treatment she turned to two old chaps and said

"Bloody hell it would be cheaper to have him put down."

"We've just had to have ours put down."

There simply is no reply to that.

But, while we are on the subject of Vet costs. Are they so outrageous? The simple answer is "no". Consider a knee replacement for a human (I worked on them for over 30 years) - what do you think that really costs considering you get it for free on the NHS? Well the metal and plastic parts alone cost about £1000 and that is for a bog standard one - add to that all the time (operating theatres about £1500 an hour) and people costs, and a knee operation, which lasts about an hour isn't cheap. Consider too, taking your car to a main dealer - I had a

Jaguar once and that was £145 per hour labour. So £50 for a 15 minute consultation including the drugs isn't so bad. And there is a big difference between looking after a Jaguar (the one with four wheels not the one lurking in the jungle in South America) and a true sentient being. I don't begrudge Vets their costs, they have worked very hard to get there (believe me it is a very hard graft) and, once there, continue to work very hard and actually aren't paid particularly well for the amount of effort they have had to put in and have to continue to put in. But I am biased of course!

We were all set. Banxie was fine, thank goodness. I called my daughter to tell her the good news:

"WHAT'S WRONG WITH HIM NOW?!!!!" she said irritably.

"Nothing, he's fine, just thought I'd let you know."

"You worry too much, he's just a bit sick, he would have got over it on his own. Did you always take us to the Doctor when we were ill?"

A fair point - £50 could buy a lot of beers - bless her, she was only thinking of me after all!

Boiled chicken and rice seemed to do the trick, and from then on, each time he threw up, which in fairness wasn't that often, I just did some cooking. I did wonder whether he did it deliberately so he got better food? It wouldn't surprise me, devious, but clever, mutt.

We managed to stay away from the Vet for a long time, but eventually we had to return. Fortunately I have been able to talk to

118

Banxie about that visit and thanks to a Dogger using Doggle Translate, Banxie himself takes up the story......

"It had been a normal day, I had been out for a walk with the fat human (FH), had a rest, had some food (same stuff) and was just dozing when I felt a bit hungry. Normally, if I do something like steal a shoe and start chewing it, the thin human (TH) gets me a treat. But everything seemed to have been hidden, which was unusual for them, so there was nothing to steal. I didn't even get my "night, night biscuit". So I went to sleep feeling very hungry and worried that I had done something wrong, but soothed myself by thinking about breakfast the next morning.

I woke up, did a bit of tail wagging and licking to wake the humans up and then off we went downstairs as normal. Out for a walk, some nice smells that morning I recall, and it had been raining, so there was that wonderful, "petrichor" scent, as it had been dry recently (get on with the story - FH). *We got back home but there was no breakfast, instead FH took me straight to the car. This was weird, and I was worried, I immediately adopted the tail between the legs pose..*

We drove along and I began to recognise the route, "uh-oh" we are going to that place that smells and is full of people way too keen to violate me. I could smell the place long before we turned in and my worst fears were confirmed. "Fuck this for a game of soldiers" I thought as the FH tried to extricate me from the back seat. Unfortunately he was stronger than me, and I did think sinking my teeth into his hand might not be a good idea longer term, so I jumped out.

Another human (AH) with some ridiculous PPE gear came out to greet me and was all smiles, but I was not having this, so just sat on the ground. Then I got so worried I peed everywhere. The FH looked really concerned and as I looked right

119

into his eyes, I really was putting it on in spades here, I felt myself being dragged away - I was heartbroken, how could the FH do this to me? I was sure I hadn't been naughty.

Inside it was not too bad actually, I was made very welcome by other AHs and was shown into a nice little room, compact and bijou. After that someone started shaving my fur, what on earth is going on? Then this tube was stuck in me, "owwwwwwwwwwwwwww" that almost got a bite from me.

Phew! Hmmm, I seem to be lying on some kind of bed, I feel a bit odd, there's a few AHs in here too, they all have masks on, I cannot see their faces, but their eyes look kind. I really do feel odd, I think I need to sleeeeeeeeeeeeeeep...........

...................blimey, that was some weird dream. And what's that pain I can feel? I'll just have a look. Oh my God, my bollocks have been chopped off. WTF?!"

When I picked him up he tried hard to look pleased to see me, but I am sure he could see the guilt in my eyes. I felt terrible, fancy making him have his "pockets picked". It was a decision we had not taken lightly and in fact he had, thanks to Covid 19, several stays of execution. There are differing views on whether to have dogs castrated in the first place and also when is the optimum time to do it. Only time will tell if we were right. (The main hope was that it would calm him down, he'd got very "humpy". But, I am not kidding, I think castration made him worse for the few weeks immediately following the operation - I was all for calling the Vet and asking for them to be reimplanted!).

We had bought a little romper suit for him in his convalescence, which allowed him to do his ablutions (by undoing it a bit) and also

120

prevented him from licking his wound. After we got him home we decided it might be a good idea to let him have a wee or even a poo - what a complete mistake that was! Undoing the romper suit wasn't a problem, doing it back up was, a major one. We must have been so naive - if you have had an operation, particularly one as sensitive as this, you are not willingly going to let people poke around in the general area are you? And Banxie certainly wasn't going to let us - this was payback time writ large.

After lots of positive reinforcement, without the positive, between the three of us (my son doing the buttoning up, me at the bitey end, my wife in the middle) we managed to get it buttoned up, but not before he had bitten me and my wife quite badly. I have this memory of him biting my hand, again I refer to "Tom and Jerry", it was how "Spike the Dog" eats a large joint of ham, or in other cartoons when they eat corn on the cob. He really did savage my hand left to right, chomp chomp, chomp, drawing blood and later bruising came out. My wife was a bit better off, that was until the next morning when he really, literally "got his teeth stuck into it", the "it" being my wife's finger.

"You should go to "A& E" for that."

"It'll be fine" she said with a Gallic shrug and a wince.

It was. Eventuallement.

The three of us decided that it was just too dangerous trying to get the romper suit back on, so we took if off, permanently. Banxie laid down on his side to show us his "crown jewels".

121

What was once a scrotum with two testicles now resembled that Viz character "Buster Gonad" (and his unfeasibly large testicles) as Banxie's wound had swollen and without the romper suit he spent ages licking it. We had to do something otherwise we would be back to the Vet fighting an infection. Reluctantly, very reluctantly, out it came, "The Cone of Shame" (COS).

I shiver just thinking about this. I think I called the Vet daily asking when we could take it off, it was like being back when he was a puppy, counting down the hours until we could undo it. The first one he demolished very quickly, and in any case it was too small and he was again free to lick his wound. Back we went and this time they fitted the correct size which worked, thank goodness. But it was bittersweet really. It drove him absolutely nuts and drove us absolutely nuts. Taking him for a walk became torture as the plastic dragged along the pavement, the constant chewing, the constant trying to get it off his head. Running repairs with duct tape, he chewed that too, I saw it in his poo. This mutual nightmare went on for two weeks, two weeks!!! My daughter said, at about 10 days, you can probably take it off now, but I was on a mission, I was going to make my life, his life and everyone else's life who encountered him a misery - and I succeeded! Everyone hated me, it, him and everyone else in the world!

The great day came and I took it off - it was as if nothing had happened, we carried on as normal. Nobody said "Thank you", Banxie did run around the garden doing a victory lap, well that's what I called it. I'm sure he was relieved, but it was a bit of a damp squib rather than the magnficent "COS-Removal-Ceremony" I had expected. After all that suffering too!

I actually shed a tear as I put the COS in the bin, I wish I had kept it as a memento of what you can suffer if you try hard enough and grit your teeth and how easy it is to piss people off. It was without doubt the worst aspect of having a puppy; puke, poo, wee, licking my face were mere bagatelles to the torture of the COS - it was even worse, last time with "Tom and Jerry", than a cat's claws running down a blackboard. Can you believe that?!! Well maybe you'll find out - be warned.

TRAINING

I once said, to the CEO of a small distributor I was trying to sell some complicated technical product to, that "you can't have enough training.". I think those words might live to haunt me - oops.

I mentioned before that I thought that Banxie would arrive loaded with "Windogs 10" or similar and, after a bit of jiggery pokery, hooking him up to the "Woof-Fi" and running a virus check, we'd be good to go. Well that's not completely true of course, I knew we had to train him, I just hoped he would be a better pupil than the other Spaniel I knew of, Nicky, my sister's pet home wrecker from the 1990s.

It was one of her daughters who said to us:

"Ooooh, you're getting a puppy, are you going to take it to puppy classes?"

"Yes we thought we had better do that, do you know of any?"

"We took ours to Canine University Natural Trainers they were excellent."

"Great, we'll try there then, thanks."

I've made that name up as I am sure you worked out, I don't want to be sued for libel..............there are four aspects to the training of Banxie, so let's have a stroll down memory lane and see how we did.

PUPPY ROMP = $2\pi\sqrt{(l/g)}$

I'm standing in a muddy car park which is full of cars, people and yapping dogs. Moments later we mobilise as one and tramp through the muddy car park to a nice verdant field. The wind is howling and so is a lady in a Hi-Vis jacket. I catch some words and try to string a sentence together which isn't easy for me as I am a bit "mutt". (I love cockney rhyming slang, and mutt is so apposite!).

"I think she said, make sure your dog has peed." I offer.

"No, keep your dog on its lead" my wife translates.

"You need a stick or two?" I said hopefully.

"PICK UP YOUR DOG'S POO!" FFS!

Semaphore takes over, which I equally cannot understand, but there seems to be some sorting going on relating to size. Ah, I see, size matters, as always. We get herded into different groups and then pointed in the direction of three different fields depending on size. Or is it age? Or is it some complicated algorithm? Finally we find ourselves in a nice little inclosure with about 15 other dogs which have something in common, not size, not age, but nutjobbery. They are all going crazy. There's pooing, biting, pissing, barking, yelping, crying, scratching, jumping, hiding, eating and probably, as Banxie is there, man-sized belching.

All champing at the bit, another Hi-Viser similar to a Hi-Viszler but with only two legs, says:

"We are going to start a game called 'Pendulum' okay? How many of you know this game?"

Nobody.

"It's very simple, just get a handful of treats, get your dog to sit down and then drop a treat to their left, and then one to their right and so on - this will calm your dog down."

Call me Mr Picky, but it didn't seem like a great "game" to me and clearly Banxie agreed. He wasn't interested in "Pendulum" he wanted to go and sniff bums and lick willies. Pendulum became more of a "shovelling food into his gob" game to keep him interested while we waited for the big moment.

"Okay well done everyone." lied the Hi-Vis lady, "Now we're going to release the dogs."

"Who let the dogs out, who, who?" I chanted.

"Are you ready? On the count of three, one, two, three and release!"

It cost £10 for about 45 minutes of unbridled entertainment. If you haven't got a dog just go to a Puppy Romp and watch the mayhem, it's far better than anything you might see on TV!

Puppy pandemonium is how I would describe it. It was hilarious and the dogs were having a ball, and so were the owners, never was so much cuteness seen in such a short space of time. Banxie was in the thick of it, holding his own, beating up Sausage dogs and Chihuahuas and taking on a great big Husky type dog called Laika. Great name.

126

("Laika" was the first dog in space, a mongrel too actually). Although Laika seemed to be a bit of a wuss considering its size. Banxie's real nemesis was another spaniel called Poppy. He'd met her before at a Puppy class, and now they were biting chunks out of each other, or so it seemed. "Just playing." the Hi-Vis lady knowledgeably informed us as litres of blood pumped out over the grassy sward. Okay, perhaps not like that but........ it looked nasty. But neither seemed to suffer any long term effects, and all the time they went back for more aggro with each other.

You know when you were young and you were told "time for bed" which you hated, well you could see the dogs feel the same when the killjoy in the Hi-Vis shouted:

"Okay everyone, start doing "Pendulum" - to the left, to the right, keep going."

Banxie looked at us - "FFS do I have to do this shite?" he seemed to say "I was just about to pull a Cockapoo."

"Left, right, left right. Release!"

It all kicked off again, previous alliances were severed and new ones made as the dogs went mad again. It was a joy to behold.

After 45 minutes "Pendulum" was invoked once again, and this time it was the final whistle. Dribbling dogs, adrenaline Mr Whippy poos and visibly shocked owners made their way back to the car park and mud. Banxie was absolutely knackered after this, it had been great fun for everyone - same time next week? Of course!

One of the critical items not to be forgotten at Puppy Romp (or indeed any training) is a box of treats. These are, as their name suggests, "special" bits of food that are given as a reward, or in Banxie's case as a bartering tool to get him to drop a sock, bra, glove, shoe etc. We were always a bit worried about over feeding him these in case he puked, and in any case did he really deserve all these rewards? A cruel aspect is that you can do a bit of Pavlovian stuff here. Simply have the treats in a brightly coloured box so that your dog associates the box with the treats and.................fill it up with his normal dog food - job done! I think Banxie cottoned onto this straight away, you could see the disappointment in his face:

"Who's a clever boy then? Good boy, here you go."

"FFS, it's a Lily's Kitchen Chicken biscuit, hardly a treat is it?"

At the first Puppy Romp we ran out of treats very early on, so had to act when we were doing "Pendulum". Unfortunately the Hi-Viser, who with the Hi-Vis jacket probably doubled up as some sneaky security guard somewhere, saw this and told us off.

"What you need is a box of chopped up, cocktail sausages."

I waited for "Take 50 lines, I must not run out of treats at Puppy Romp."

"And you also need to give him more treats during the 45 minutes."

And this was something that really got up my nose about Puppy Romp. Considering we were the customer, we were made to feel very inferior. I know it can't be easy running this type of thing but it seemed to me there was a lot of "pissed with power" going on. And the patronising tones really didn't help. Eager not to get detention next week, my wife added "Industrial Size Box of Cocktail Sausages" to the weekly shop (I was happy) and off we went the following Saturday (with a trailer for the sausages) confident that we wouldn't run out.

Banxie must have thought all his birthdays and Christmases had come at once. Actually he wouldn't have thought this at all because he is a dog. Nevertheless he would've clocked the enormous volume of treats in the box. Puppy romp commenced with the, by now, irritating call for "Pendulum" and the associated dropping of millions of treats. As time progressed the sausage mountain decreased until they had all gone (admittedly I had helped Banxie a bit with this project).

There's only one thing that is going to happen here isn't there? Yep, the sausage mountain made a reappearance on the way home, all over the car. I guess it was inevitable, but the Hi-Viser knew better naturally. At the next Puppy Romp, I was on my own with Banxie and gave him boiled chicken treats and again got mocked for the paltry poultry I was dishing out. The Hi-Viser got on her sausage mountain to deliver the "Saveloy on the Mount" speech but I cut her off by explaining that he had thrown up last week so we were feeding him bland food. I could feel the Hi-Viser looking down her nose at me, probably thinking I had gone for cheap sausages rather than expensive ones. She knew best of course.

We took Banxie to Puppy Romp for a few weeks and he loved it. So did we, apart from the patronising and being made to feel inferior. But all good things come to an end and eventually Banxie got a promotion, or a red card depending how you look at it. Not for doing anything bad but just for being a bit too bouncy, a bit Tiggerish. A Hi-Viser took us to one side and said she'd been watching him and noticed he was getting bored. We had to admit that this did seem the case, he wasn't as thrilled and mad as he had been at the start, I guess he'd sniffed enough bums and there wasn't an obvious new "bum pool" coming through. The Hi-Viser told us that we would have to stop bringing him but we could enrol in another class - "Recall". This sounded excellent, and would provide a good additional bit of training to the Puppy Classes we were already attending.

PUPPY CLASSES

Canine University Natural Trainers ran the class that we enrolled in. The first week we attended without Banxie, so that we could learn what would happen over the next 8 weeks, what we had to bring etc., etc. It was a bit like ante-natal classes without the lying down and controlled breathing. The lady running the class didn't sport a Hi-Vis, and actually, seemed rather shy and retiring, definitely not "pissed with power". Just as a digression, Dog Training appears to be a very sexist job, no blokes at all, surprising given the number of Hi-Vis jackets available.

I had expected the class to be in a room the size of a Sports Hall, a bit like Cruft's, packed with enthusiastic dog owners. Instead it was a relatively small room and there were only 4 couples there. At least we would get close tuition I thought.

A week later we pitched up and immediately saw a flaw in the location. Or perhaps I should say a floor. A nice shiny floor. We entered the room, Banxie copped the other dogs and made a beeline for one of them. Again I refer to "Tom and Jerry" - his legs were moving frantically, but he was going nowhere, slipping and sliding all over the place. Comical. The other three dogs suffered the same fate.

We introduced ourselves.

"Banxie, Sprockerpoo, basically an expensive mongrel."

"Max, Viszler."

"Autumn, Beagle."

"Willow, Cockapoo."

131

"Poppy, Psycho."

The trainer welcomed us and then ruined the entire next 8 weeks by saying:

"Let's start with a game called 'Pendulum' okay? Do you know this game?"

Everyone in the room fearing the worst, including the dogs, reluctantly said:

"Yes" and muttered "Fuck no, not again, please."

"Okay everyone, let's calm our dogs down with "Pendulum" shall we?"

And off we went, left, right, left, right, but it wasn't "Pendulum", it was just the owners trying to grab hold of the dogs as they ran around instead of sitting obediently on their mats. It was mayhem once again.

"Okay everyone, let's calm our dogs down AGAIN with "Pendulum" shall we?"

All this did was give a brief period for the dogs to refuel before they all went nuts again.

A few weeks in and to be honest it was pretty boring. We did the same thing over and over again (yes I know that is how you train animals) and then some weeks there would be a promise of new stuff the following week, but that didn't seem to happen. "Recall" kept on being mentioned but I only remember doing this once. But it was quite memorable.

We had been trying to train Banxie, in the garden, to come back to our call. He was actually pretty good at this; I could just whistle and he would come back. The trainer explained she would hold each of our dogs and then we should walk out of the hall into the corridor and call them.

I went first and good old Banxie came straight away, his happy little face smiling.

"Well done Banxie, everyone look at Banxie."

I was going to burst with pride until in full view he pissed on the floor. And, to make matters worse, ran off to inspect the toilets and the cleaners servicing them, they loved him, he had a great time. Eventually, in his own time he returned to the class, and of course "Pendulum" was invoked to calm him down. Left, right, left, right, "Can we go home now?" his face said, and so did mine.

The evenings were actually quite enjoyable really, although I am not sure, as owners, we learnt anything particularly new, but it was good reinforcement of what we were doing at home and there was the aspect of socialising for the dogs. But in truth it was pretty hopeless to expect there to be any real seriousness to the training with five puppies desperately trying to meet each other and have fun rather than be interested in schooling. It was basically an hour of treats and disobedience for them. We were pleased that Banxie actually seemed to be the most well trained of the five, he was good at tricks, and on the rare occasion that he actually listened to us, he would sit on his mat while we walked around it, or would leave his treat until we said "Go". That was encouraging, and for once we felt we were doing the right thing. We didn't get told off at all, and I think the Trainer actually had a soft spot for Banxie.

We attended all the classes, Max the Viszler showed no commitment and left after a week, but Autumn, Willow, Poppy and Banxie, the class of late 2019, made it through and got a certificate and a discount off another Canine University Natural Trainers' course, such shameless, but obvious marketing.

We had ticked two boxes; "Romp", done, "Puppy Training", done. One left for us three, "Recall", probably the most important command for a dog. When your dog goes AWOL, chasing sheep, horses or other dogs, or cyclists (well not to worry about them too much) you need it to come back on the command of "HERE!!!" or when you call its name or blow the whistle.

Well good luck with that then.

RECALL

This is how the dictionary defines the verb "recall".

1) Bring (a fact, event, or situation) back into one's mind; remember.

e.g. "I can still recall the trip to the Vet."

2) Officially order (someone) to return to a place.

e.g. "the French ambassador was recalled from London."

3) Term used in dog training that doesn't feature in Banxie's vocabulary."

e.g. "HERE!!! BANXIE! HERE, NOW!!! BANXIE, BANXIE, HERE!!!"

In 2011 a video of a dog called "Fenton" running amok with deer in Richmond Park was posted on YouTube, it went viral. I know just how that bloke felt.

So it was back to the even muddier car park with the Hi-Vis festooned Canine University Natural Trainers for a spot of "Recall Training". Four weeks, each Saturday afternoon, aimed at getting your dog to come to you rather than have the time of its life running after interesting animals.

Back in the mid 1990s the company I was working for was expanding, and one market that it was seriously sniffing was France. Hello! I have a French wife, hello? Could I wangle a job in France perhaps? It was unlikely but, just in case it happened (and this sparked many rumours), I was given two weeks off to attend a crash course in

135

French in London with Berlitz, the famous Berlitz. Up till then my French had been O-level standard. Okay I lied, I actually got an 'E' so it wasn't even pukka O-level standard, but had been improved by visits to my in-laws. My wife really should have been better at teaching me, *"reinforcement positive"* wasn't one of her "core competencies", impatience was though. Just before I went on the course, I remember standing in the kitchen at home and saying to her, naively optimistically:

"It's going to be strange talking fluently with your family."

Two weeks of torture ensued. I had hoped that it would be two weeks of conversational French, but no, it was back to basics.

"Comment t'appelles tu?"

"Darragh."

"No, no, no, please, it's 'je m'appelle Darragh'."

"But you wouldn't say that."

"You do here Garçon."

The only happy memory I have of this exercise was seeing Sir David Frost on the train - I was allowed to go First Class and he almost, almost sat in my compartment. Sadly he didn't but I did manage to piss on his cigar butt that he had left in the loo.

I still can't really converse with my in-laws after 30 plus years. Yet, naively optimistically once again, this is what I thought would happen with "Recall". It was that "Windogs 10" moment again. Turn up, do the stuff, job done! If only.

136

We had bought a lead that seemed to stretch into next week for the class. The idea being that the dog is free to roam but ultimately you are in control and when you call, you can reel them back in. Eventually they make the connection, "hear call, go back for treat". This is the theory. The practice is somewhat different.

Very early on we decided that we had made a mistake parting with £70 (less £5 because Banxie passed the other course) because it did seem to be a bit "couldn't organise a piss up in a brewery." Worse still, the very first thing to happen, and there was a collective sigh from owners and pooches alike, was:

"PENDULUM!!!!"

Oh FFS no, please no.

Left, right, left, right. Banxie looked at us "Really?" Eventually the clock stopped ticking and we were into "Recall" good and proper. We were lined up in the middle of the field, and told that alternate people would walk in opposite directions. So A, C, E would walk East, and B, D, F would walk West. When you got to the end (of your tether), you doubled back round to the starting point and joined a queue to start again. A and B set off with a Hi-Viser each, and it was the Hi-Viser who had the lead and was in control (who else?!!) walking with your dog while you walk on ahead. The absolute critical instruction was "DO NOT LOOK BACK, KEEP WALKING" and the Hi-Viser would call out when the dog was close and which side they were on, so that you could just put your hand down and give your dog a treat.

Seen from above, this could have been something choreographed from a Busby Berkeley musical. At ground level it was hopeless. The whole thing made the assumption that the dogs would be so unhappy that they would follow their owners in a straight line. What a poor assumption! You have a puppy in a field with lots of other puppies, new smells and treats all over the place that have fallen from the previous class - what could possibly go wrong?

With Banxie, who by then had become pretty hopeless at recall, it went like this from the Hi-Viser; she was the only one allowed to talk of course:

"3-2-1 go!!"

"Don't look back!"

"He's coming up on....no he's not."

"Don't look back!"

"Now he's... nope."

"Don't look back!"

"Yes left, no right"

"Don't look back!"

"Oh he's gone off left, no right, now left."

"Don't look back!"

"He's, er, um, he's, well he's oh, don't look back!"

We got to the end of the walk and eventually Banxie arrived, and then ran off to inspect something else.

"Oh well done, very good, go and join the queue and we'll do some more."

Well done?! It was rubbish, the only winner was Banxie who got a ton more treats than he truly deserved. Back to the queue and nobody knew whether they were A,B,C,D,E or F such was the organisation. There seemed to be dogs all over the place, and Hi-Visers shouting at each other:

"Are you going that way?"

"No, I'm going here."

"But you're A aren't you?"

"No I'm B now."

"Yes but B goes that way?"

"Eh?"

"I thought you said you were B?"

"I am."

"But you just said 'A' "

"Oh, no that was 'Eh?'.............as in what the fuck is going on?"

It was awful and we had four weeks of that. Did Banxie improve? He can't recall.

ON OUR OWN

Pretty much since we got Banxie we started to train him. My wife buried her nose in a couple of books, and we had plenty of advice from other people who had, or had had dogs in the past, oh and plenty of advice from people who had never had dogs at all. I had the spectre of my sister's Cocker, Nicky sitting on my shoulder and hoped that our combined efforts, as well as the classes, would result in a superbly trained, mega-obedient delight to have around the house and as a companion. And then I woke up from that dream and saw Banxie staring at me while he bit my fingers.

We gave everything a go from basic stuff like "sit" to the more advanced "wait", while we walked off. He actually wasn't too bad, but I noticed that he seemed to have a lot of fleas when we did training, he was always scratching himself, especially with the "wait" command. A quick look on Doggle revealed, much to my dismay, that this could be because he was nervous, or worse, that I was a shit trainer. On holiday in France in 2010 I was playing Pool with my son, trying to teach him how to hold the cue and how to play some shots (I am not very good at Pool, I admit). A guy watching us, out of nowhere piped up with:

"Youer, nart ah ferry goude teachair."

I wanted to say "mind your own business" (this is "encule toi" in French, look it up) but I was really hurt. Sadly then, I appear to have form as a bad teacher. Nevertheless I persisted and eventually Banxie got quite good at "wait". But he did seem to have some random number generator app running during these times as he would be consistent with waiting, only to then spoil it all by scratching and running off.

My wife taught him some tricks and soon, to an assembled audience, he was able to sit, lie down, roll over, one paw, other paw, and high five for his reward - not bad. However we didn't want a circus act, what we really needed was a dog that wouldn't jump up at people, would walk to "heel" and would, when you called out "Banxie", come running back.

A year later we are still looking for that dog, Banxie it is not. He isn't always hopeless, in fact most of the time he is okay. But he suffers terribly from distractions, or as someone pointed out, they're actually attractions - true that. We've tried too. Our kids give us (well me really) some real abuse about Banxie's obedience and the criticism hurts, just like that Pool situation in France all those years ago. I feel as if they think we did nothing, or rather as I look after him the most, that I have done nothing. Yet we did try, we really did, we did everything that we learnt at Puppy Training, much of which we were already doing anyway, and also tried to improve his recall. But self instigating "Pendulum" was a step too far for me, I had to go and lie down at the mere mention of the word.

I did notice that if my wife was with me, Banxie did appear to behave slightly better, or so I thought. But as time has progressed I've realised what it is - I am more relaxed when there are two of us; I am

141

not 100% responsible, we can share duties. And perhaps because of that, so is Banxie. Rather than get all het up about things, and get really worried when a person or another dog comes within a million miles, I've changed. And I am getting more and more comfortable with it - and, dare I say, I think Banxie is getting better. Now that I understand what is going to happen I can prepare for it. If we go for a walk and other people appear, generally he will ignore them. Before I would race around to get him on the lead, now I don't. It doesn't always work but in fairness people are incredibly understanding about him, and nobody has got in the least bit shitty about him if he has jumped up.

I always apologise too, I'm not one of those dog walkers who instantly shout abuse when I've been criticised - it's fair game, I feel, if Banxie annoyed them. Next up are cyclists. Banxie used to chase them, which might have annoyed them but he is used to them now and these days I just let him run, if they have to brake or stop then good. They are without doubt the most selfish users of public spaces, never has a cyclist stopped for Banxie and me, we always have to be the accommodating party - gits. More gits later too.

Other dogs. I think the etiquette is, if another dog is on a lead then you should have your dog on a lead. This works well. I have no problem if Banxie is on a lead and there are other dogs running around, unless they are smaller than him. I am reluctant to let him off even if the owners say "it'll be fine" - experience tells me it is fine for a few seconds then Mr Tigger gets really bouncy and there's yelping and gnashing of teeth - it's not a pretty sight. And you can see the surprise and regret in the other dogs' owners' faces. Same size and bigger is not a problem, and in fact is a great laugh - "instant walking" I call it and two dogs go mad. It's actually pretty impressive watching the speeds and agility that dogs have and Banxie is superb at this.

Children. Absolutely on the lead. I might ask them if they would like to "Say hello" to him, but I always make sure they're not frightened. Banxie is not that big, but he is bloody strong and has no idea of his own bounciness. It doesn't always work though. Once, on Patch No 1, Banxie was roaming around when he espied a lady with (what I assume were) her Grandchildren. He ran off to inspect them and just would not come back to any amount of calling or cajoling. I ran after him and as I got to them I heard:

"Just keep still, keep absolutely still and we will be fine."

I felt terrible. I managed to get hold of him, apologised profusely and waited for a well deserved stream of invective. Amazingly the lady was very polite and calm and just accepted it was "one of those things with puppies". I got off VERY lightly here, I can't imagine I would have been so generous if the tables had been turned. Eventually the frightened children got to pet Banxie and, luckily we parted on good terms. What a lovely Granny!

Walks have changed in this year from a fraught, nervous exercise, worried all the time that he will do something wrong (he did in heaps!) to a much more relaxed time. I know he will come back, but "recall" is on Banxie's terms at the moment. He just needs to investigate the attraction, whether that be another dog, a human being, a cyclist (they're not human) or a dismembered animal (yep he's found those on several occasions, not humans thank goodness) so I let him get on with it and so far we haven't had a fatal attraction. I've definitely grown to love him a lot more since I took the rod out of my arse.

DOG IN DA HOUSE

We are lucky, we live in a nice house in a nice area, and for a relatively modern house, it has a decent sized garden. Neither of us are keen gardeners, but we do maintenance type stuff so it looks good enough. Inside, while it might not be to everyone's liking, we think it's nicely decorated and my wife, sexist though this is, keeps it immaculately clean. I say sexist but in actual fact the truth is I am not really allowed to help cleaning. I could do it but I know that two minutes later my wife will be in to do exactly the same thing. If I protest then I will be told I haven't done it properly. This extends to pedantry when it comes to loading the dishwasher. A plate could be moved one place because "it wasn't in the right place".

"But it makes no difference!" I protest.

"Yes it does." End of conversation.

Strangely her mother is like that too with their dishwasher, weird these Frenchies.

Just before Banxie arrived, we discussed what he would and wouldn't be allowed to do in terms of access to the house and garden. The garden is fenced-in so he could have "access all areas" there. We would just have to keep an eye on him with regard to the pond - dogs, particularly spaniels, like the water. Inside was a different matter. We would set the crate up in the kitchen and he could also have a bed in the kitchen. Pretty much the rest of the house would be "off-limits" unless accompanied by a responsible adult (not me then). You have to

145

admit, this was excellent planning wasn't it? Top notch. How come then, it all went so horribly wrong?

The phrase is "too soft", way too soft. Plus, a dog who moved at the speed of lightning and was able to become invisible at the slightest hint of incarceration. After not very long, Banxie took on the form of Genghis Khan and ruled great swathes of the house. Any attempt to take back territories was met by defiance and naturally, biting. Not savagery, just gentle needle like reminders as to who was the boss in da house.

We did have some success though. In the "Curious Incident of the Crate in the Late Evening" we won and Banxie, reluctantly, conceded that this was the best place to sleep. Phew!!! There were one or two instances when he barked and barked but we stood our ground, and it worked! Sweet slumbers and dreams. But it didn't last. As Banxie grew, so the crate shrank, and what had been a nice little apartment became just too small, so we bought him a nice brand spanking new detached house. It was lovely, well we thought it was. Banxie had other ideas and after an all too brief spell, decided he would take advantage of Rishi Sunak's Stamp Duty holiday and move.

The move came as a bit of a shock. All had been fine but one night barking commenced. Despite "shushing" him from upstairs, which normally worked, he would not be quiet. In retrospect, now we know, it's possible he was spooked by a Fox or a Badger, both of which have been seen outside. Whatever, he wasn't happy. Downstairs one of us trotted, unlocked the crate to be greeted by a very happy bouncy dog. "Can I come upstairs, oh please, please, please let me." Who could resist, and up he came, jumped on the bed and settled down for the night. And he's stayed there ever since. Attempts to rehome him have been futile, he's glued to the bed, it's his territory now. The crate has been consigned to history and neither of us has had a good night's sleep since. Actually that is not true, I have, when I went bird watching on the Isles of Scilly for a few days.

A typical night starts off okay, he's well away from us, but as the night draws on Banxie uses the bed like a chessboard making moves all over the place, with a great deal of thought in between each move. Long enough to allow some slumber to occur but not much before being rudely awakened. Towards dawn inevitably I will wake to either feel or see his arse in my face, thank God he doesn't fart much, and as it gets lighter he will slither across me and stick his elbows in my crotch. That's my first alarm call, for various reasons. He will then proceed to lick my face, yuk again, and then stand up and crush my chest. All the time wagging his tail as if to say "Good morning FH how are you today?"

"Broken and tired." I think.

I will give him some credit though, he doesn't wake us up really early, he is quite a slumberer himself - 08:30 is not unknown. In the summer it is worse. He gets hot and so every 30 minutes or so there is a thud as he jumps off the bed to go and lay down on the wood floor

147

which is cooler. Once he is cool, there's another thud as he jumps back on the bed and wakes both of us up. When you get your dog, no matter how much it barks at night DO NOT GIVE IN. If you do, your life will change immutably. And I haven't even mentioned the dirt.....

I think all dogs moult, some more than others, so we were expecting to find hairs all over the place. Actually there weren't as many as we thought there would be, which was nice, but what the house lacked in fur it made up for in FILTH. I am not talking porn here, unless you have a fetish for mud. Bloody hell, I wasn't expecting that. Even a quick trip on the decking resulted in tell-tale footprints everywhere. And that's not including any crap that he picked up on the way. I'll tell you how bad it was, and this is going to shock you - I started hoovering and my wife didn't complain - that is serious right?

It didn't help that it was autumn when we first got him, so the first 6 months were wet to say the least. One of the annual activities that I have to do is gather up the leaves that fall from two enormous oaks. I hate doing it, but I have to do it. Firstly I take the leaves out of the pond with a big net. Next I rake up the leaves around the edge of the lawn and then finally, if it is not too wet, I get the lawnmower out and hoover them up. With Banxie at large in the garden it was a little bit different. For some reason Banxie took a real shine to the fishing net I used. I had to hold it high to avoid him jumping up to grab it. I couldn't always keep guard and unfortunately when dropped he was in like the proverbial rat up a drainpipe, chomping it and ripping it. I did learn a new skill though, "net repair".

Banxie doesn't like the lawnmower (it is a petrol one) so goes off to do something else which is normally sniffing or digging. Sometimes he digs "off-piste" which is fine, but unfortunately the lawn is his favourite area. Goodness me he is the JCB of the canine world. Recently I took him on a walk where three guys were putting up a massive "Berlin Wall" type fence. Now, can you get excited about fences? Well I can, and I stopped to admire the construction and have a quick conversation with the guys building it. Banxie was bored shitless so decided to do what he is good at, digging. Very quickly he dug a large hole.

"Can we hire him to dig the holes for the posts?" said one of the guys.

"Yep, three Kongs a day."

Banxie wasn't impressed with the deal.

The lawn was never brilliant, far too much moss, but now I look at it and am pleased to report that the moss has gone..........and has been replaced by holes. So what was once green grass (and green moss) is now green grass, dead grass and muddy holes - Capability Banxie has been hard at work.

Leaf duty done, in we went for tea and medals with Banxie dripping leaves, mud and bits of fishing net all over the kitchen floor. If I was careless and left the gate open, he'd make sure that the kitchen floor wasn't singled out for special treatment and cover all other floors in the house - very quick he was at it too!

As longer, drier days arrived, the mess did actually subside a bit so we could relax when he went outside. Or so we thought! A new problem or game (depends whether you are me or Banxie reading this) arose - pegs. Taking the washing in became a nightmare because if he was able to grab a peg he would. This wasn't funny - they were plastic or wooden, which isn't too much of a problem, but they have that nasty metal spring in them. My "worrying" mode jumped to a vision of Banxie on an operating table with the Vet extracting a peg with a tea towel attached (he loved them too) from his stomach. Fortunately this so far hasn't happened. Much as he likes pegs, tasty treats are better currency, but be warned!

Anything made of cloth like material is fair game for Banxie. You can always tell when he has something because he runs head down and hides, tail wagging with a face that says "Ha, ha, ha done it again losers!" So far I think he has taken shoes, socks, pants, gloves, bras, knickers, tea towels, hats, cushions, mats, rugs, pegs, t-shirts, homework (ho, ho), books, magazine, newspapers, bog roll (as mentioned before) and even his own food bowl. His food bowl, which bears the brunt of his chewing, twice a day, looks as if someone has run it through with an AK47. It's as if he can't stop eating once he's finished his biscuits.

I remember he stole one of my work shoes once. Lovely brogue in brown leather. It was so sweet, he wasn't much bigger than the shoe and it was an effort for him to walk with it. But off he trotted, under the bed. It can't have been more than 3 minutes later that I took a little look. I think I saw a shoe, I am not sure though. It was reminiscent of what Banxie had in his mouth a short time ago, but very different - bastard!

Generally the treat "con" works, and the target of chewing can be removed, but not always. Sometimes he is really possessive about his "chews". I don't like wrestling with his jaws, particularly when he starts growling. But so far so good, apart from the bollocks incident of course.

The reason he steals these things, apart from getting treats, is for chewing. Again we were ready for this, dogs chew to help relieve pain when their teeth are coming through and as they get older it is a way of keeping their jaws strong and teeth clean. Based on this, I can only assume that Banxie is an obsessive in the world of canine dental hygiene. He chews for England (or France). He chewed from day 1 and he is still chewing. We've lost count of the number of toys he has got through. Seriously, some manufacturers need to look at what they are putting out. I've seen him demolish a toy in a couple of minutes, one that is meant to last ages during "puppy teething". Like hell it does.

There are a couple of toys that have really stood up though, a green bone which he has had trouble wrecking and a blue bone shaped thing. There was also a white one but he's almost got through that now, but it has done well. Mats and rugs are one of his favourites. Rubber backed ones a speciality - chew spit chew spit chew spit. Everywhere! And bits of rubber mat in his poo where he forgot to spit, well at least it didn't linger. Without doubt his worst spot of chewing was when he was young. We were in the lounge and he was still small enough to hide under the sofa. All was quiet for a while until there was this little "nom, nom, nom" noise indicating something was being chewed. Hmm, what could he be chewing under the sofa, nothing too bad we hoped.

I looked under and saw to my horror that the nom, nom, nom noise was Banxie chewing the electric cable to a standard lamp. OMFG - get hold of him. Banxie was having none of this and squeezed himself further away from us, all the time looking like some hideous teenager chewing a bit of gum. Nom, nom, nom he went. Surely it was only a matter of time before yet again a "Tom and Jerry" moment would happen with a bright flash and a dog shaped piece of toast burnt into the floor? Out came the treats, and eventually the teenager dropped the cable and we grabbed him. It sounds funny now, I can tell you it wasn't at all.

So chewing is a big pastime for Banxie. I have read that he may be chewing because he is bored, mildly anxious or frustrated. I sincerely hope not - I am pretty sure he has a lovely life, I think the only reason he chews is because he just loves it.................and it's good for annoying humans.

The only credit I will give Banxie is this: he has never chewed the furniture and for that I am eternally grateful. He might have wrecked

152

everything else, made the house filthy on numerous occasions, dropped fur everywhere and dug up the garden, but the furniture has been left alone.

For now.

STUFF AND GETTING STUFFED

There's lot of gear you can get for your dog, tons in fact. And there's lots of people happy to take your money and sell you rubbish. That applies to almost everything! My wife and I decided to have a competition and see how much we could steal from Marks and Petsers - she took the lead early on. B'dum, tschh, thank you.

Briefly here's a list of some of the things we bought and what was and wasn't useful, oh and also some words about..............food, glorious food.

Crate - I think I have done this to death. Very useful early on and if you are hard-hearted it is essential. If you are soft shites like us, then probably better not to waste your time and just let your dog sleep on the bed from the start.

Collar - Definitely get one of these, you'll need it for both of the next items.

Lead - Lots of different ones to chose from. We have used a choker (good if you want to strangle your dog, awful really, but you don't even need a collar for that one), a couple of what I would call conventional ones, and an extendable one. The Canine University Natural Trainers banned the extendable ones which was fair enough because with the mayhem of Puppy Romp the field would have ended up looking like a massive and somewhat ironic "Cat's Cradle". However I didn't agree with their view that they should be banned full stop. I use the extendable one quite a lot because it gives Banxie the false

154

impression that he has freedom so he doesn't pull so much. The only downsides are that he has a habit of going the opposite side of any obstacle we encounter (although he has learnt to loop back) and they can get badly tangled and therefore damaged. I regularly check to make sure it's tickety boo. One other piece of advice, if you do buy one get the "strap" type lead not the "rope". I got a nasty burn from one when another dog decided to investigate Banky's arse while wrapping himself around my legs. Bloody hurt!

One thing I just have not mastered is attaching the lead to the harness or collar. If I had the inclination I think I would try to design something that was far simpler for me to operate. I just cannot get to grips with it. I can feel Banxie's frustration when I am trying to attach it, I think it won't be long before he says "Give the damn thing to me, I'll do it!" - no idea why I struggle, see how you get on though!

Harnesses - There is a massive amount of bullshit about these. Guaranteed "no pulling" ones are the worst. We have three different harnesses, all of which Banxie hates and none of which prevented him pulling. However, they're preferable to putting a lead on just a collar in our experience. The problem with Banxie is that if the harness only has a lead attachment on the back, the harness around his shoulders gives him a massive mechanical advantage and he can pull not with his throat but with his shoulders. Banxie isn't huge but he's incredibly strong, strong enough to pull both of us over on different occasions. So get a harness that has an attachment on the chest, this helps reduce pulling,

155

but be prepared to be disappointed when your dog spoils the strapline "no pull guaranteed"!

Stair gate - This is absolutely essential if you want to imprison your dog so you can go off and have a rest. There are loads of different ones, but make sure you have one that has a double action latch on it. The one we have has a mechanism whereby you have to squeeze and lift to open the lock. Unfortunately it can be put in a position where only a lift is required and we have fallen foul of this on many occasions as Houdini has made a break for it. I can guarantee I can find him straight away though, under our bed eating bog roll. The only thing I don't like about the stair gate is that I am the only person who can't step over it, FH short arse that I am.

Toys - Like training, you can't have enough toys! Your dog will chomp its way through loads. Be careful of squeaky animal toys. Once ripped to shreds, as will happen, your dog will find the squeaker. I have managed to rescue this from Banxie on a couple of occasions - it's a bellows made out of plastic - not great and I am surprised that such toys are available. Be warned - if you suddenly see a crocodile, some sausages and hear Mr Punch you know what's happened.

Train your puppy books - Nah! My wife did read a couple, I browsed.

Portable Shower - What a great piece of kit this is. Ignore the specific "doggy shower" ones, they're just there to rip you off, just get the Hozelock one, or similar, for about £30. It is perfect for washing

156

the mud and shite off, and you can either take it in the car or have it strategically positioned at home for when you arrive back. If you think you don't need one then that's fine. You will.

Car Seat Cover - Your dog will ruin your car's interior believe me (Aha, but not if you take the Portable Shower with you!). If you go for a walk when the ground is anything less than bone dry I guarantee your dog will find some mud and water somewhere. Once back at the car you will either have a wet dog that jumps in and puts mud everywhere, or, if it has been a long walk and sunny, you will have a dry dog that jumps in and puts dust everywhere. My car is a cross between an IRA muddy protest and a vehicle that has been on the Paris-Dakar rally - awful, thank God it is old.

My wife came to the rescue here. A bit of Googling found these wonderful big covers that attach behind the headrests of the front and back seats - if you had it tight enough it could be a hammock for your mutt! These are great, you just unhook them take them out and put dust everywhere! No seriously, well worth having.

Towels - You will definitely need many of these!

Poo Bags - I have mentioned these before, just don't buy coloured bags.

Kongs - These are rubber cones that you fill with something edible. The idea is that your dog will spend time trying to get anything out that is trapped inside, or will lick everything it can reach. They come in various sizes and are excellent - can't praise them enough!

Well I have segued into the real business, food. Oh, your dog is not food orientated, okay, well ignore this bit then. Here are some of the things that we have fed Banxie and how he has rated them:

Anything vaguely edible 🐾 🐾 🐾 🐾 🐾

I jest......though many a true word said in jest. My experience of feeding dogs is that they basically ate everything that they could get their snout into. Those days are long gone apparently. No more white dog turds on the pavement, chocolate not allowed and definitely no alcohol. The dogs of today have no idea of the life lived by the likes of Waggy and Ben.

Let me expand on that a bit. I can sit here and write this and quickly get transported back to those Christmases and New Years of the 1970s. Certainly very different times back then. I have a memory of one particular New Year's Eve party at my sister's house, when she invited some quasi-relations of my Mother's. Nice people who seemed to have a rather weird "science experiments" streak in them. I can't believe this happened, and I confess I was party to it, but I distinctly remember giving Waggy shots of Vodka and Whisky. It was not unusual back then to give chocolates to dogs either. Milk Tray, Terry's All Gold and Black Magic were firm favourites, although I remember even the dogs turning their noses up at the toffees left in a tin of

Quality Street (which was twice the size it is today) - dogs imitating humans eh?

Waggy spent the next day under a chair, paws on his head nursing a hangover - oh how we laughed! Isn't that shocking? Not that we laughed, but that we gave him alcohol? He probably had alcoholic poisoning! It seemed like the thing to do - a good laugh. I am ashamed that I was involved, yet I can't recall anyone saying that we shouldn't be doing that. Different times, terrible times if you were a four-legged Heinz 57. Or did he have an absolute blast?!

As far as I am aware, Banxie hasn't eaten any chocolate nor have I caught him having a sneaky snifter behind the garden shed. Saying that, he eats most other things. As time has progressed so then has dog food, the stuff in packets and cans and also the stuff that isn't packed - e.g. on plates at home. I am terrible at this and I confess I have fed Banxie from the table. Tut, tut, but I only did this because I thought it would stop him moaning. It did temporarily until he'd eaten the food and came back for seconds. The dishwasher is also a prime target for him. As you open it to put something in, particularly cutlery, he is there licking anything he can get his tongue round. I have given up trying to push him away, he just won't take "No!" for an answer, but I am cautious if we have had a "Fiery Goan Curry" for example as I don't want him to experience the canine version of Johnny Cash's "Ring of Fire".

The other thing he does, of course, is practice to be on "Dogsterchef". This he achieves by "helping" when we are preparing food. His help consists of putting his paws on the work surface and angling his neck such that he can nick anything within reach or, helpfully, clean off the work surfaces. He really is such a bad boy and I really am such a bad owner! When he was young he couldn't reach, and it was actually cute seeing him with his paws half way up the cupboard doors and his little tail going nuts. Now when I cook I generally get a chew ready or a Kong, that keeps him occupied, for a while.

So what does he eat? I have been quite surprised by his diet, food I would never have thought dogs would like he seems to love. Sometimes we try out new stuff but not before we've Doggled it, to see if it is safe. Here's what he loves:

Everything that we are eating.

Dog biscuits.

Wet food.

Anything the cat eats just to be churlish.

Sardines.

Anything with the word "treat" on the packaging.

Anything with the word "chew" on the packaging.

Sweet potatoes, mashed - absolutely loves this in a Kong.

Peanut butter - loves it as a blob on a chew, or in a Kong.

Crisps and peanuts - tsk, tsk, not very often.

Spaghetti Bolognese, or indeed any pasta dish - yummy.

160

Rice.

Boiled chicken - I always boil some for the pets when I cook.

Apple - sometimes, he is a bit Marmite about apple.

Marmite - he is a bit apple about Marmite.

Carrots - he is a bit Marmite and Apple about these.

Rabbit Ears - ultimate treat, keeps him occupied for a while too.

Mango - a little bit.

Raspberries.

Peas.

French Beans.

Pork pies, Sausage rolls and a Mortadella sandwich which the bastard nicked off my plate when I wasn't looking - on three separate occasions of course!

That'll do. He's a very good eater and very rarely leaves anything, on our plates, they look pristine afterwards, no dishwasher needed! Seriously, he does eat well and even though his hormones have gone mad since being castrated he hasn't put on any weight - he is still lithe and lightning quick - particularly when the dishwasher is open.

Long term chews. On a few occasions we have given him bones from the butcher and also once, an antler. The antler was astonishing value for money, it lasted months. The bones also lasted a long time, in fact both items would have lasted even longer were it not for the torture of hearing him eat them.

"Oh look at him with his bone, such a good boy."

Graunch, crunch, nom,nom, nom, crunch graunch ad infinitum.

"Oh my God get the thing off him it's driving me mad."

Much growling and snarling.

"Okay you can keep it."

Graunch, crunch, nom,nom, nom, crunch graunch ad infinitum.

THE NUMBER OF THE BEASTS

Well it's five, not 666 - I am talking about other important animals that have featured in Banxie's life. Actually there are another five, but they're wild, they'll be livid after Banxie sees them; I will save them until we get out and go walking, coming up soon, stay tuned.

The beasts are Jack (BSJ) and Todd, as you may have expected. But there's also Shamus, Pilot and Clover. Who they? You'll find out in a moment, but first let's deal with the two "old timers".

BSJ- Banxie has met Jack on a number of occasions. Remember that Jack is much older, he must be pushing 10 or 11 now, and therefore, as he is also a boy, he is much grumpier. If we use the totally incorrect calculation that one human year is seven dog years, then Jack is well into his dotage, so it is not surprising he might not be too keen on some young whippersnapper encroaching on his lifestyle. It's been an okay "friendship", nothing too bitey, but sometimes quite growly. Banxie assumes anything with four legs will want to play so just bounds in and says:

"Hi Jack, shall we play?"

"Bugger off."

There's some mutual bum sniffing but because Jack is so close to the ground, Banxie can't go overboard with the welcome and lick Jack's willy - this is a good thing, Banxie can be a bit over friendly at times, well all the time really.

We've taken them on walks and that has gone okay, providing it's all on Jack's terms. There's quite a lot of "buggering off" and definitely any stick is Jack's - that was made obvious by the quick snap that Jack made at Banxie early on. Banxie ran off, tail between the legs, trying to look cool, but not.

"Okay Jack, how about we run together then?"

"Bugger off."

"Okay Jack, how about I just disappear into the background and leave you alone."

"That works for me."

TODD - Todd is a tad younger than Jack, but I don't think the same stupid formula works for cats. If it does then Todd is a reasonably cheerful mid 60s cat. As cats go he is remarkably tolerant. Originally he was a birthday present for our daughter when she was 16, but when she left home to go to University, our son firmly took over the reins. Todd is very much his cat now, and I do wonder if there is actually a bit of "therapy" going on there - it's not easy finding a job as a recent graduate of Journalism, (with a "First"! - proud parent moment 2.0), in these bizarre times. Todd and I have a rubbish relationship, he is only interested in me when he needs feeding and to be honest I am only interested in him when...........er, well I am not. As I mentioned before I accidentally dropped him when he first arrived at home so he has never forgiven me. He is a very handsome cat though, I will give him that.

164

When Banxie first arrived he was a little bit smaller and much slower in terms of speed and reactions than Todd. Todd ran the show, Banxie didn't get anywhere near him. It was never nasty, Todd was too quick for that. It wasn't until Banxie began to grow that things changed. My abiding memories of these two are Banxie, paws up on the kitchen table where Todd is sitting, Todd with his ears so far back they are on his tail, hissing, spitting and adopting the orthodox stance, leading with his right paw stretching it, claws out and embedding it in Banxie's face. It's as if he needs to scale Banxie's head and he is using his claws as crampons. It looks nasty, and I think it probably is!

This is followed up by what looks like a circus act - Banxie placing his head inside Todd's mouth, or so it seems. What it actually is, is Todd distracting his jaws, snake like, and embedding his teeth into Banxie's head. It's fucking hilarious! So good I have videoed it several times. I am not sure if it is just "fun" or something more serious? They both come back for more, time and time again. Then Todd will get fed up, jump off the table and there is mayhem as Banxie chases him up the stairs.

There are two destinations: under the bed or on it. Each has a very different outcome. Under the bed, where Banxie can't get to him, results in a load of barking, a responsible adult coming up stairs, a grabbing of the collar, a load of bitey stuff (admittedly playful, or that's what I tell myself as he is gnawing my hand) and removal of the offending canine.

On the bed...........OMG, it looks like carnage. Normally by the time I get there Banxie has his face stuffed up Todd's backside, nudging him. I have no idea what he is trying to achieve. Or his face will be in Todd's chest, nudging him. This is bad because it means Todd is able to wrap right around Banxie with all claws deployed into various part of his anatomy AND is able to bite chunks out of Banxie's head. It looks awful, but it's fucking hilarious 2.0.

Either we manage to separate them or Todd makes a run for it.......back downstairs and onto the kitchen table. You know the rest.

I'm not sure whether they like each other or not, so far no lasting damage, although the wooden varnished stairs look a bit grim. No blood though, well not yet. What is it about cats and dogs? Why or how do they know they have to perform like this? The dog's head in the cat's mouth is without doubt one of my favourite memories of Banxie's first year with us - cruel though that sounds, but so funny.

SHAMUS - While we were researching and interrogating the owners of Banxie's parents, my sister was embarking upon a very different canine adventure. She'd decided to act as a trainer for a "Hearing Dog" - that's one that deaf, or partially deaf people use. Just as an aside I am constantly amazed at what dedicated trainers can do with dogs (clearly not my core competency, more like my core incompetency) such as Guide Dogs, Sniffers etc and I take my hat off to them, tremendous work indeed.

166

She passed muster and was on the recipient's list. You don't get to choose the name, they are chosen in strict alphabetical order and so you're lumped with the name whether you like it or not. Shamus could have been so much worse - Spencer, Sadie, Summer and Skipper so she escaped there I feel. I've probably just upset loads of dog owners. Shamus is 75% Working Cocker Spaniel and 25% Show Cocker Spaniel, or as my sister's friend's young son said "Oh look it's Shameless the cock-up dog." I am always amused by "Working Cocker Spaniel'" is there an "On the dole Cocker Spaniel" or "Sorry, out of order Cocker Spaniel" I wonder?

Shamus is a few months younger than Banxie and is therefore a bit smaller than him, and always will be. Once Shamus was old enough, and allowed to meet other dogs, we thought what a great idea it would be to meet up and take them for a walk together.

Bear in mind that Shamus is on a strict training course and my sister has to carry out specific training each day and is regularly audited on his progress. My wife and I were also very interested to meet Shamus too, so we went to see him, without Banxie, when she first got him. He was very cute, although I couldn't help noticing that it seemed as if someone forgot to colour his nose in properly as he had a pink dot on it, nothing that a Sharpie pen wouldn't cure. The next time I saw him it seemed fine, was that a receipt from "Staples" I saw in my sister's waste bin?

The great day arrived and my sister suggested a venue. Given Banxie's form in the obedience world and given too, that Shamus had been on a very strict regime where training was concerned I hoped that when they met there could perhaps be a "Little Britain" moment - Kenny Craig the hypnotist. I imagined Shamus and Banxie meeting and Shamus staring into his eyes and saying:

Look into my eyes, look into the eyes, the eyes, the eyes, not around the eyes, don't look around the eyes, look into my eyes...you're under, you're going to be the most obedient dog in the world from now on, 3, 2, 1, you're back in the room.

We got them out of our respective cars and they met for the first time. Leads at maximum tension their eyes met and.............

Look into my eyes, look into the eyes, the eyes, the eyes, not around the eyes, don't look around the eyes, look into my eyes...you're under, forget all this training shit, come with me and I'll show you a great time mate, 3, 2, 1, you're back in the room.

Oh fuck no please.

"Are you ready to let Banxie go?" My sister enquired.

I was still shocked by what I had seen.

"Okay, 3,2,1 and GOOOOOOOOOOOOOOOO."

A white arrow pursued by a slightly quicker brown one sped off into the distance, met and crashed. It was havoc. Banxie was so violent and despite telling Shamus he would have a great time, it appeared anything but. Shamus was great at recall, which meant Banxie followed him. Shamus was good at stopping too, Banxie just bowled straight into

168

me and bounced off. And then they were off again. It seemed to be a game of "savaging the neck" a game for two players only one of which does the savaging - Banxie, naturally. My sister could see her Hearing Dog becoming an ex-dog so we tried to get hold of them both. There was a lot of jumping up, a lot of panic, a lot of snarling and a lot, lot more running and biting. Well I say biting, I don't really think it was that bad.

"He's trying to dominate him" My sister said as Banxie continued to try to take great chunks out of Shamus's neck.

"Oh, looks like he's succeeded." I said, as Banxie stood arched over and firmly gripped to Shamus, pumping for all he was worth.

We separated them, put them on their leads in the hope they would calm down. And they did! Remarkable. Phew! After a few minutes walking on leads and a decent amount of treats we decided to give it another go.

Mistake! It all kicked off again. More savagery. Eventually it did calm down and they began to be okay with one another. But then something would happen, maybe a stick was found that they argued over, or, more likely, Banxie got his nose too close to some delicate part of Shamus's anatomy and it all kicked off again. After an hour of this we decided we'd had enough and took them back to the cars. The only positive thing was that both dogs were totally knackered.

So much for a rigid training scheme.

"He's never been like that before." said my sister relieved but somewhat shocked, also saying one of the greatest lies in the world.

"He's never met Banxie before."

That nightmare has been repeated weekly, and even though both dogs have now had their "pockets picked", the carnage continues. But I'll tell you what, it isn't all Banxie. Shamus can be a little fucker too.

PILOT - My late sister's older daughter, following in her mother's footsteps, was desperate to get a dog. Not content with three kids and a business to run she felt that a bit more stress would be a good thing. My niece is extremely precise in her life. She is a good cook but if it says "35 grams of butter", it must be 35g exactly. I imagine she did a ridiculous amount of research before getting a dog. In fact I know this because our daughter was consulted on numerous occasions. My niece always wanted a Black Labrador, which she got, right after she finished her PhD in "Dog Selection: Optimisation of Family Values and Canine Requirements." She chose the name "Pilot" - quite a good name I thought.

My niece lives in the South West of England and as I had to pick my daughter up nearby and Banxie was at home I thought it would be a good opportunity to go and meet Pilot. Because of "lockdown" Pilot had not been out much or at least had only been socialising with the five members of the family. Intruders weren't really welcome because he wasn't used to them. So sadly, well irritatingly really, he just looked at me and barked. Things would calm down, but then something would

170

make our eyes meet and off he went again. "STFU!" I thought, but didn't say in front of young ears.

My niece suggested going out in the garden. We sat down at a table and she brought out tea and biscuits. "Aha" I thought, using my profound knowledge of dog behaviour "I know what'll stop him barking." I picked up a biscuit, broke a bit off and offered it to him. The reaction was not what I expected, but it didn't come from Pilot, he was happy. It was my niece:

"WE DON'T GIVE PILOT HUMAN FOOD!"

I tried to process "Human Food" and realised she meant "biscuit". Blimey!

Banxie hasn't met Pilot yet. This is a very good thing indeed. I am dreading it when he does, which inevitably he will. I think I will refer to that great organ "The Beano" to give an analogy. It will be like "Dennis the Menace" meeting "Walter the Softie", I can see it now as Banxie takes Pilot off to corrupt him.

Look into my eyes, look into the eyes, the eyes, the eyes, not around the eyes, don't look around the eyes, look into my eyes...you're under, when you wake all you'll want is Human Food, 3, 2, 1, you're back in the room.

It doesn't bear thinking about.

There is actually one other animal of interest that Banxie met, but just once. One evening we met up with the owners of Banxie's parents. The husband was doing us a favour - plumbing in a tap. He asked if his wife could come and see Banxie and so we suggested they bring Clover too. Clover is actually Banxie's sister, and was the one of the litter that nearly died, the husband resuscitating her - top bloke. As she was so lucky to survive they thought they would name her "Clover" as in four-leafed - sweet.

Dogs, (it may be all animals) don't do this sibling stuff. Clover could have been anybody. It was difficult to see how they could be brother and sister - they didn't look anything like each other, she was far more Cockapoo than Banxie (so took after their father). And so nervous.

I knew this couldn't really be his sister though, she was so well behaved.

WALKING ON SUNSHINE AND DON'T IT FEEL GOOD!

I do apologise, I got side tracked on all those other issues. But here we are, we are ready to do some serious "walkies" (Barbara Woodhouse, bless you). I am convinced that this is the major reason why people get dogs. (I am reluctant to say "buy", it still sounds so awful and vulgar). You know right from the start that the dog will require walking, so there is a commitment there, or at least there should be. And surely this is one of the most rewarding parts of dog ownership - out in that big wide world watching them run and run and run - and Banxie certainly isn't a slacker in that respect. It is, believe me, THE reason to get a dog, particularly if you had a lifestyle as I did, mainly sedentary - "working from home".

So where do we start?

The routine that existed when he was young has changed considerably now, and I feel it is for the better. I think he is used to this and seems to be happy with it, as much as you can tell if a dog is happy with a routine, what a stupid thing to write!

For Banxie the routine starts quite early as my wife is up by about 7am while I am trying to "push out a few last zeds", having spent the night working out if Banxie is moving "Queen to Rook 5" or "Knight to King 3" or still trying to mate me.

His first walk of the day is the morning constitution, which generally my wife does, after which he has his breakfast (biscuits and a Kong) while my wife and I discuss whether it was a "formed" or "Mr

Whippy" kind of morning. My wife goes off to work and Banxie is left alone in the kitchen for a while. This is really the only time he has to suffer on his own, and even then it isn't that long, it depends on what I have to do in my busy day!

One of the most important things I have to do is to work out where we will be going for our "big walk". There are many options, but I can categorise them as follows:

1) (GC)^2 - This is our local walk, the Green Church and Golf Course - I love this walk, it takes up to 2 hours and I find it fascinating observing the minute changes that have taken place in the world each time we do it. Three cigarette butts today, there were only two yesterday, somebody has walked here since us yesterday. Fascinating! We do this one 2-3 times a week.

A brief diversion (already?!). I knew this before, but walking Banxie really hit it home to me, and that is the unbelievable amount of litter that is strewn across our land. It really is disgusting, from bottles, to needles, gas canisters to tissues (millions of those and Banxie loves them, eurgh), to takeaways, human puke, car hubcaps, balloons, sandwich boxes and my personal hate, cigarette butts. Smokers are disgusting litterers, they really are.

What these people (lazy ignorant gits) don't realise, mainly because they don't give a shit, is that this detritus may be harmful to pets not to mention our native wildlife. "Keep Britain Tidy" might have been a dull government initiative, but it was and still is true - we need to stop throwing stuff away.

2) The Forest - This requires a drive but has lots of choice, although I normally stick to a few main routes - also the different routes are dependent on the time of year as bird watching is a big feature of this walk.

3) The Seaside x 2 - Another car drive but two nice options "to be beside the seaside, beside the sea".

4) Patch No. 1 - This can be either a car ride or a longer walk, it takes in a beautiful river and open grass areas lined with Poplar trees.

5) The Downs - Another car journey, but well worth it, probably my favourite walk.

There are others but these are my main routes. I try to jumble them up a bit so Banxie, or more likely me, doesn't get bored, but to be honest does he care? No of course he doesn't, he is just happy to be out discovering new smells and reacquainting himself with old ones.

I did say at the beginning of this part of the book that I felt it would be boring just to relate the walks we did. Hopefully up to now you have agreed with me. Well, humour me for a while, because now I would like to take you for a few walks and tell you about what we see, who we meet and most of important of all, what Banxie makes of them, or perhaps what I make of Banxie as he runs around like a lunatic.

Before we go, we have to go through a checklist to make sure we have everything and are not "at home to Mr Cockup" as Blackadder might say. It is season dependent but this is the list

Poo bags.

Treats.

Poo bags.

Can of lemonade (that's for me).

Poo bags.

Treats.

Water (if it is hot).

Binoculars.

Poo bags.

For goodness sake, don't forget the poo bags!!!

Once I've checked off this lot I'm ready for action - if it is summer then it's straight out of the door, but in autumn, winter and spring I am most likely going to have to put on my walking boots because it is so muddy. Walking in these times is a bit of a pain, but experience has meant that I can largely avoid the mud. Experience has also taught me that no matter where I go Banxie is incapable of avoiding the mud.

Talking of which, I forgot something in the check list - load up that portable shower and put it in the garage ready for the return. In the summer he still gets covered in crap but I use the garden hose on him, he seems to like that, cools him down I guess.

The next bit would make the "Japanese Tea Ceremony" seem like a two minute wonder, it is the "Lead-and-Harness-Putting-On-Ceremony". I mentioned earlier that sometimes I think Banxie is a fake dog. I was under the illusion that ALL dogs liked going for a walk, well this one doesn't. Or at least he doesn't like the preamble. Whether that is something that happened in the past (I think it is, I will explain later) or he simply hates the way I faff around, who knows? All I know is it takes a geological era of time to get his harness on as we dance round the kitchen table, me trying to catch him, him doing his level best to avoid me. He looks so miserable with his tail between his legs, and a couple of times he has even weed. Once or twice he has been compliant but normally I have to put on an Oscar winning performance to show him how sad I am, put the harness over my arm, pick up a treat and attract him that way. That normally works. If we go in the car it is much easier I just put the lead on his collar and put the harness on later as I have him trapped there!

After a couple of hours, he is harnessed up and ready to go. For this first trip we are doing the $(GC)^2$ route, so the car is not involved (thank God).

Out we go.

Bollocks I've forgotten my 'phone. Now you may be identifying with this. It is a fact of life these days that we don't like being anywhere without our mobile 'phones. They are incredibly useful and incredibly irritating when they are being useful for someone else. And I expect

177

you're thinking that not having my 'phone with me is worrying me in case I need to contact someone urgently. There is some truth in that, but it isn't the real reason. The real reason is at worst OCD, at best anally retentive, and I blame one of my bird watching friends entirely....

I am standing by a big gorse bush, which acts as a windbreak in the Forest. It is getting dark, it is damp and it's cold, it's Winter! I am with the aforementioned friend who has his telescope set up, we are both "binoculared" and Banxie is running around trying to tip over the telescope and generally annoy my friend. Much to my surprise and pleasure he welcomed the chance to meet Banxie for the first time, about 2 hours ago, but I feel his magnanimity has dwindled somewhat, and after being licked to death and jumped up at he's probably approaching "I wish that dog would piss off." territory. But he has a brave face showing. We are looking for a very rare bird indeed (more so these days as they are regularly shot out of the skies by grouse hunters), a Hen Harrier. My friend surveys them in the Forest.

"I wonder how far Banxie walked today compared to me?" I muse out loud.

"Hmm, dunno, but, let me have a look, I've done 10,000 steps so far."

"Have you got a pedometer thingy then?"

"No it's just an app on my 'phone."

"Really?"

"Yes look."

178

"Oh, I must have that on mine too then."

And that was where a big mistake was made. So the reason I MUST take my 'phone is not because of some emergency, well not a medical one at least, but I have to make sure I record all the steps I take. It is a fascinating thing to me and the source of much derision from everybody else! But it is a useful indication as to how much exercise Banxie and me are getting, and I am really pleased that my monthly average number of steps has increased more or less throughout the year he's been in our family. And I've lost a stone in weight too! What a result!!! I must've done well over 300 walks with Banxie and according to my "app" (which appears to rob me of at least 500m every day if I compare it with internet maps) I have walked over 800 miles with him - I am really pleased about that, not a bad effort at all. The one thing that was a bit depressing though, was the fact that on looking deeper into the app, I saw that the data went back a few years. Some days there were hardly any bars on the charts. I felt ashamed. My wife had often said "You need to go out at lunchtime if only for 15 minutes." - but I never did, and there was the evidence to show me. No wonder I am FH.

One item I really should buy is a GPS for Banxie - it is on the cards - I reckon he does a minimum of twice as far as me, and perhaps as much as five times the distance, maybe even more - fascinating don't you think?

Can you see how much I faff? No wonder it gets on his tits.

179

Before we go out on $(GC)^2$ there's one very special walk I want to tell you about. This took place on 10th November so just under 2 weeks after he was first let out into the big wide world.

We are standing in the same Forest, it is a lovely autumnal afternoon and Banxie is having a good sniff.

"Okay, ready?"

"Yes, I'm really nervous though."

"Why?"

Can you work out why? I'll let that marvellous Astronaut Neil Armstrong tell you:

"This is one small step for a dog, one giant leap for Banxie."

I bend down and unhooked the lead.

"Are you sure he'll come back?"

"Of course he will, he's too much of a wuss not to."

And that dear reader is the end of the story - we never saw him again.

Only kidding!

I am not sure he could understand what was going on and perhaps couldn't believe his luck. You could see him thinking "What? No lead? Really? Can I?" And like a scene from "Born Free", Matt Monro's dulcet tones blasting out, off he went. Banxie unchained. And he loved it and so did we. He would run off leaping like a miniature gazelle, so when he was lost in the bracken all we saw was this aerial Spaniel - it was hilarious.

We walked for quite a way until we reached a long path. I suggested that I walk ahead and see if he would run to me. I reckon it was a good 100m if not more. My wife held him and I shouted "Banxieyyyyyyyyyyyy". Fortunately I have it on video, but what a little star. Running like a little brown arrow with his luncheon meet tongue hanging out, almost smiling. Peeeeeeowww he zipped past, stopped and came to me - brilliant! He got a well earned treat, and then with my wife calling "Bankzzzzyyyyy" (because she is French and can't pronounce "sy") he made the return journey. We did this until he was tired out. He was a star, 100% recall! Arnie would be pleased with him.

I look back at this and think "Why did his recall ability go so badly wrong?!

Back to $(GC)^2$ - we are out the door and heading up the drive. Banxie surveys the large lawn of the old people's home and sniffs the air. He can probably smell cats and dogs, not to mention wild animals Grey Squirrel, Fox, Deer and Badger, he's already excited. We have to negotiate a couple of roads, "Sit", treat, "Cross", and then we are on the Green Church path. The Green Church always confirms to me that God simply doesn't exist, otherwise he wouldn't have let it get into such a state of disrepair, it's awful. But we move on and our first important stop is outside Daisy's house. Daisy is a Dachshund owned by the sprightly 80 years old Gill. Sometimes we see them, but more often than not, we don't. Banxie always looks forlorn if they're not there. It's at this point, if the gate to Gill's house is closed, I let him off the lead. If the gate is open then Banxie just buggers off in search of Daisy.

On we go down the path which, at this point, changes name to "Yappy Dogs Lane". Banxie has his eyes to the sky looking for squirrels. We normally see them (Grey bastards, unfortunately) and he jumps up on his hind legs, like some giant Meerkat, as if he's going to launch himself and grab one. So far he's been too slow, but I can't help think it is only a matter of time. Then it's past the house with the three yappy dogs and then onto another house with two yappy dogs, none of which we ever see, but that scare the shit out of Banxie with their yapping. He has to go back on the lead as we walk through a residential area and just to keep me on my toes Banxie doesn't walk in a consistent manner. There's out in front pulling to the left, out in front pulling to the right, behind to the left and behind to the right. And of course in front pulling to the left quickly becomes in front pulling to the right but not before he's done both sides at the back, which means my right hand is now wrapped behind my back. Either I switch hands, which I am loath to do in case I drop the lead (which has happened and is a horrid experience if he realises and runs off in the road) or I do a rather fetching twirl to redress the balance. Banxie must know somehow that I hate "Strictly Come Dancing" and does this deliberately just to wind me up, literally and mentally.

After a bit on the lead and a good nose at the houses to see if anything has changed, we pass a cottage named after a battle in

182

Afghanistan in the 19th Century. I had no idea about this until I talked to the owner as she admired Banxie's coat:

"What a beautiful colour."

"Yes it is, lovely chestnut." I lied, remembering I wanted a black dog. Chestnut?

We then get to "The Pointless Gate", a memorial to the inept Borough Council. You have to see it to believe it, or.....just watch "Blazing Saddles". In that wonderful film, there is a scene where the dumb cowboys come across a "Toll Crossing" in the middle of the desert. That is all it is, just a crossing with desert all around it. To pass they simply have to ride around it, but exemplifying their stupidity they search for money, pay the toll, the barrier lifts and they're through. "The Pointless Gate" is a standard "gate to a park" design, a sort of kissing gate I guess, but it stands alone. You can walk either side of it. It is utterly ridiculous and no matter how many times I see it, it annoys me. Such a waste of we taxpayers' money. Fume.

We then scale "Mount Million Pound House", a hill that runs by the side of a house originally on the market for £1m. It didn't sell for that though, but the name stuck. I used to let Banxie off the lead here, but in recent times he kept running off to discover whether a £1m lawn was more or less diggable than our own. I keep him on the lead until the summit which has the benefit that he pulls me up. At the top he is off searching for more squirrels and scent marking like it is going out of fashion.

I stop to admire the "Berlin Wall" construction where Banxie was offered employment as a JCB and then we drop down the other side of MMPH onto a slightly secret path, which I am keen to keep secret. Banxie will be lost to sight by now as I take a slight slope upwards and emerge into the open, a few hundred metres from the fabulous international sports stadium - there's a hotel within the complex and, as I quite like my architecture (or what I know of it), I stand to admire the design - very modern, very cool. A great place to watch sport. And if your sport is spotting white vans then this is the place. Probably 100 or more congregate here each day to talk about the state of Britain's roads and the ever increasing amount of traffic. Actually they are something to do with Amazon's distribution network. What is worrying though, is that there are a lot of Hi-Vis jackets around. Banxie clocks this and we look at each other.

I mouth "Pendulum?"

Banxie mouths "Fuck right off, and when you have, fuck right off even further."

Fair comment.

We wave at the drivers and the "Check-In" people, they're probably delivering dog food to our house. Good people! We walk on to the massive open area of grass and recently planted saplings, which affords a fantastic view over to the Downs. If I scan hard I can normally pick up a Common Buzzard or two or even Red Kites. Mind

184

you, you can see these almost anywhere now, such is their common status.

Banxie is delighted to get to this bit, so am I, because his behaviour becomes comical. With a backdrop of white vans, the Downs and the stadium Banxie sets about investigating the unkempt area around the saplings. I can only assume that the area is covered with mice, rats and voles, that has to be what is so compelling to him. I suspect I could stop the walk right now and just stand there for a couple of hours and he would be fine with that.

Firstly he gets down on his front paws and snorts along the top and inside the grass. Following that, he rears up on his hind legs and then leaps in a lovely arc onto.............nothing. He is like an Arctic Fox in the snow, without the snow. His success rate is zero. For live stuff. For a dead mouse, it is 1. I knew he'd got something because he ran off in his sneaky mode, head down, ears down and looked like guilt personified, well dogified I guess.

Naturally the whole thing turned into a not very funny game. Banxie was thinking "this is fun, FH has no hope of getting it off me" and I was thinking "Emergency Vet Admission". Every time he swallowed I winced, more crap in his digestive system. It took an age to get hold of him, positive reinforcement was put on the back burner, but I did eventually manage to grab him. Next was like something out of a wrestling match as I tried to prise his jaws apart. He was having none of it. Incredibly strong. He wasn't going to be the one to give in, no way!

185

And then I hit on an idea. I remember, vividly, the lecture "Mouse removal from Canine Jaws" when I was reading Engineering at Uni so used that insight to help. I dragged him over to some trees, found a decent stick and stuck it in the more proximal part of his gob. This shocked him as he couldn't now grip the mouse. That done I gripped the mouse's tail (thank goodness I had gloves on), yanked it out and threw it over a fence and pond into the wilderness - gone forever.

I gave him a treat (why FFS?!!) told him he was a naughty boy and onward we went. A nanosecond after the treat, he did a 180° turn and ran off in search of the mouse. The look of disappointment on his face when he realised the smell emanated from beyond water, which he hates, not to mention an unjumpable fence, was to behold. "You bastard." I could see him saying, "I was enjoying that."

We walk on down the path by the golf course (the second GC) and around the 18th hole, quickly nip across the 1st fairway and round to a bench on the 2nd tee, this is our only rest spot. Again a lovely view, across a large lake lies the 2nd green and it is my little piece of entertainment to sit here, sort through the gulls in case there's something rare, and watch the golfers try to beat the lake. I played quite a bit of golf in the 1990s (but not these days) and this course is so beautiful I will simply have to get my clubs out and play here one day. It would be rude not to; judging by the number of "plops" I hear and see, I won't be out of place in the skill stakes.

Banxie couldn't care less about golf. So, to while away the time, he digs up the area under the bench. An inane session barking at the motorised trolleys and carts and it's time to move on before we get in trouble. From here we generally retrace our steps back to the "The Pointless Gate", but of late an unforeseen benefit of "Lockdown" has appeared - no golf allowed. We sneak behind a hilly fairway and knowingly trespass all over the course. It's brilliant! Banxie runs and runs and runs. I keep him off the greens, he seems to know this is not good etiquette, but bunkers are a different story...........oops. Fortunately, as far as I know he hasn't shat in one, so he has some modicum of decency. His recall is actually pretty decent here without any distractions / attractions. If I call him he pretty much always comes back for a treat. When I say "he comes back" this is a slight lie. Banxie seems to have a "that's good enough for me" app that runs all the time when out walking. So "coming back" means he got within 10m, showed his face and then ran off again, occasionally coming back the whole way for the said treat.

Although his name is officially "Banxie", I do call him by other names. I have no idea why this is, but it makes no difference to him, he just needs to hear a two syllable noise to know that he must ignore me at all costs. Sometimes I call him "Banquo" (I hope he doesn't think I am going to have him murdered), sometimes "Banks" and if I am really trying to get him to cheer up "Banxie-boo" (OMFG where did that come from?). I have probably confused the hell out of him with this,

187

added to which he probably thinks his name is also "Oi", "Hey" or "Ah, ah, ah, don't do that". No wonder he's as mad as a balloon.

Once I have had my fill of breaking the law, and inspected the lakes for anything decent in the bird world (Grey Heron and Egyptian Geese the pick) it's either back to small mammal hunting for a while, then the ascent and descent of MMPH through "The Pointless Gate" and back home via a slightly different route where we pay homage to "The Battle of the Bone", or I can extend the walk through the woods. First the violent battle - this is similar to the mouse incident. Banxie picked up a bone that had been thrown away by some evil person and would not let me have it. Treats didn't work and this was before my innovative engineering trick. In the end we were grappling on the side of the road, again it looked like a wrestling match. Eventually I managed to get it off him and we continued walking, just as a car drew up. The lady driver put the window down:

"Oh, you're alright, oh thank goodness. I saw you with him lying there I thought he had been run over and you were trying to revive him, so I wondered if you needed any help. Are you sure it's all okay?".

I confirmed it was and explained that far from being run over and being revived I had been fighting the little git. But, whatever, how nice was she to drive past, see the entertainment and come back to check all was okay? Makes you feel that there are still some decent human beings out there.

188

The route back through the woods covers areas that when I first walked Banxie I walked in some detail. This was before I started to make the walks longer as he grew up. During "Lockdown" we did the "wood walk" every day - I never got bored and of course Banxie was more than happy. It's always rather fetching (sorry about the pun) to see him lead the way. Generally I enjoyed this walk, the weather was normally kind and most of the mud had gone. I noted how many bird species I saw - 52 in all, including 30 in a single day - wonderful! But on one occasion it was completely unpleasant. I was inspecting the golf course for anything interesting when a noise behind me grabbed my attention. Turning round Banxie and I both came face to face with two Rhodesian Ridgebacks. At the time they were much bigger than Banxie. His first move was to "Say Hello" which gave rise to a chase. They disappeared to be replaced by two blokes walking towards me and a chilling howl from the woods.

"Your dogs are attacking my puppy!"

"No they wouldn't hurt a flea."

The phrase "total bullshitting lying fuckers" entered my head. Those two meant business. I could hear Banxie crying so went to locate him. I seriously thought I was going to find half a dog, mangled beyond recognition. What I did find was terrible but not how I imagined it would be. Banxie had been running in the chase and his collar had caught round a branch and presumably yanked him back and kept him trapped. We were mutually pleased and relieved to see each other. I released him, put him on the lead and regained the path, with Banxie happy as anything, wagging his tail and looking generally unfazed by the whole thing.

Two guys were looking at me, the phrase "total bullshitting lying fucker" coming into their minds. I had the grace to apologise - and they were fine. Magnificent well behaved dogs too!

The walk passes without further incident, although at any time now we might meet Mark the Postman. Mark is such a nice guy and Banxie really likes him. Sadly his friendliness towards Mark is rather shallow because Mark has a bag of biscuits on his person at all times, essential if you are a Postie I guess.

"Would you like a biscuit?" Mark asks.

"Is the bear a Catholic?" Banxie mixes up his jokes because he is so excited.

We move off, bidding a "nice day" to Mark, Banxie has a nose at a new house being built (this is a total lie, it is me who is interested) and shortly we are arriving at home. Harness off, he's reasonably clean so no shower, into the kitchen and he is straight into his bed. This is not because he is tired, it is because he knows he is going to get a Kong. Sweet potato and peanut butter never tasted so good.

And that's $(GC)^2$ - I love this walk, there's a lot to see, even if some of it involves a bit of trespassing. But hear this. Coincidentally the very day that I wrote this I did the $(GC)^2$ walk and saw one of the Groundsmen coming towards me in his buggy. I was prepared to

190

apologise and get off the course, but, yet another decent human being, he tells me "Don't worry mate, we like dog walkers, keeps the other idiots off the course." Result!

Depending on what time we do the daily long walk, Banxie will have one or two wee walks, wee by purpose and wee by distance. I then sit down at the kitchen table with my spreadsheet and feed the numbers in:

$$\text{Minutes of exercise per day} = 2 \times (5 \times \text{age in months})$$

Hmm let's see he's now 8 months, so that 80 minutes a day. The walk has taken us two hours, we are way overdrawn at the "Bank(sy) of Walking". But then I think what a load of bollocks this is, by the time he got to 12 years old he would need to be exercised 24/7. Ah, but it is only for puppies, so there is a cut-off. I give up on this and just ensure that he gets a decent amount a day, which I am sure he does. Mind you, I think he would just go on and on if he were allowed to - amazing things Spaniels.

Going for a walk that requires a car is a different matter. Or at least it was. When Banxie was young it was easier not to take him in the car by a mile. Not only did we have the "Lead-and-Harness-Putting-On-Ceremony" to contend with we then had the "I'm-not-going-sticking-to-the-floor-Ceremony" malarkey. It was the Alchemist's reverse dream, a lump of gold becoming leaden at twice the weight. He just wouldn't budge. Eventually one of us would carry him to the back of the car and strap him in. This would result in a very, very miserable looking dog (dropped ears, wide eyes, hatred staring me out!) and a very dribbly one. Treats were no good. I am not sure whether this was because he was being miserable or he was genuinely feeling sick. Eventually we would drive off and all I could see was his chin resting on the back of my seat dribbling all over my clothes. When we got to the destination the mess in the back was awful. But Banxie was happy, he'd jump out, wag his tail and say "What?". Such an actor.

But then we thought we had cracked it. We were driving about 200 miles in two legs to see our daughter, which included an overnight stop at Pilot's house, but before Pilot arrived. Worried that we would have drowned in gob by the time we got there, we consulted our resident Vet who recommended we get some travel sickness pills for Banxie (I think that's code for "knock-out" drops). We needed three to cover all the journeys, bloody £18 they were, what a rip-off. Anyway, tablets taken off we went and a miracle occurred, Banxie was well behaved. He just hunkered down and we didn't hear a peep out of him. Pills popped for the journey back and 200 miles was a breeze. As a reward I took him to the Forest the next day, to his favourite spot where he first went off the lead. Fantastic no problem at all in the car. I called my sister to tell her the good news, so that we could meet up somewhere other than locally.

The next day I got him ready and we were back to square one. Dribble, dribble, dribble, everywhere. And then I realised why. The drugs had been so effective he had probably still been "under the

192

influence" that next day! Poor little soul. Thus ensued a very long time of dribbling in the car. "He will grow out of it.", lots of people said. And, do you know what? He did! While I wouldn't say he is raring to get in the car, he has now been dribble free for months and even, can't believe this, will get in the car of his own volition. It certainly makes for a happier start to the day.

The second time I ever took him for a walk was to the seaside. I admit I wanted to have a bird watching session so told him that he had no choice. Apart from the pre-walk ceremonies everything was okay........except just one thing. And I think this is significant in his little world. He would not stop jumping up. I got more and more angry and I, in a "positively reinforcing" manner, told him to "stop doing that!" It really got on my nerves. I look back on this and think "oh shit, I got that seriously wrong.". I've been told that one of the reasons dogs, and in particular Spaniel breeds jump up, is because it harks back to their collecting prey (e.g. shot birds) and bringing it back to their "master". That may be true, I am not convinced. But when I read, at a much later date unfortunately, that jumping up may be because they are nervous and worried, my heart sank. What an utter bastard I had been to the poor little soul. And I can't help but think that this is why he doesn't like the water. He associates it with an unpleasant experience. I could be completely wrong and he really is just a fake dog, remotely controlled by someone else, but I don't think so. I think I have a big burden to carry there. So, if your dog gets on your tits, jumping up all

193

the time, spare a thought for the longer term game, it might be worried, and you might cause it more grief by getting pissed off.

The Forest walk is always brilliant whatever the season and weather. Unless it is windy. I bloody hate the wind, I can deal with heat and wet but wind - bugger off will you! Banxie doesn't give a stuff about the weather which is a good thing, although I try not to go out when it is raining cats and dogs - ha, ha!

In the Forest there is a lot to see from a nature point of view, and I must admit my attention to Banxie does drift a bit here. Birds are plentiful with some real stunners at certain times of the year (Honey Buzzard, Redstart and Spotted Flycatchers in Spring, Great Grey Shrike and Hen Harrier in Winter and Goshawk all year round) but there are also butterflies, dragonflies, a bit of botany and reptiles and amphibians. I often wonder if people are truly aware of what you can see if you look hard enough.

There are also animals in the Forest, Grey Squirrels (bastards), various species of Deer, (we will come back to those on another walk) grazing cattle, pannaging pigs and my least favourite, ponies. I hate them, sorry. Big four legged animals that weigh a third of a ton and run using a random number generator - totally unpredictable and bloody dangerous. I once saw a pregnant woman get kicked over by a pony, not pleasant and an ambulance had to be called.

It's Boxing Day and we are back in the Forest at the place with the pond where we took BSJ all that time ago. There is a nice walk through the woods and out onto the heath. We park, I see the resident Mandarin and a Goosander for good measure, the weather is good, we are all happy (I am in a really good mood as it is 26th December so Christmas is about as far away as it can get). Off we all trot, Banxie trying to play with BSJ, BSJ telling him to "bugger off" all is well. BSJ goes off piste, Banxie follows. We call them back. BSJ, obedient as ever (code for shit scared of his owner) trots back as does Banxie until he clocks something far more interesting out of his eye - a pony. It is that "Waggy" moment from the 1970s repeating itself. I can see him weighing up the situation. With Waggy it would have been "is it worth a smack to get to chase a pony?" With Banxie it's "so they've been told about positive reinforcement, is it therefore worth a few treats and a 'lovely boy, good boy, well done Banxie, you scared the shit out of us, made us run miles, but you are such a good boy that you came back on your own terms 10 minutes after we started calling you' to get to chase a pony?"

No brainer. That's Banxie!

He's off.

I think Mack Sennett and the Keystone Cops would have been proud of us. Five people running around achieving little towards the goal of getting Banxie back. And all the time dreading what surely would be inevitable. A nicely timed hoof would be no match for Banxie's precious snout. It didn't bear thinking about but his mortality was firmly fixed in my mind.

195

Miraculously the pony did nothing and just trotted off. For a split second I loved that pony. And in fact I have a grudging respect for them now, as we have had several encounters, this was actually not the worst, that came later when he was much older. It took even longer to get him back and there were even more ponies. We have ridden our luck many times - or rather he has. This is the one big problem with his recall. With other dogs he just wants a bit of play and as we walk on he will catch us up. With ponies it is a whole different ball game - they don't want to play, he gets annoyed, starts barking, they get annoyed etc., etc. how he hasn't had the shit kicked out of him I don't know.

I still go to the Forest regularly, I am about to go there right now, and I am still apprehensive. But two things have helped. One is that I tend to know where the ponies will be, so am mega-vigilant, and secondly, the dreaded extendable lead, hated by the Canine University Natural Trainers, really helps. He feels he can have a bit of a sniff at them and I can keep him under control. It is a "work in progress" but my heart rate is better these days.

I've saved my favourite walk till last - the "Downs". God I love going here. Something always happens! I try to do at least one walk a fortnight, sometimes with Shamus - that's always high-octane stuff as they run together, trying to bite chunks out of each other, as usual.

We first did this walk years ago before Banxie arrived on the scene, (you know, normal times) and I thought it would be a great, if long, walk for him. The walk is about an 11 km circuit and you can choose to do it either way. You can also chop off a bit too if you are feeling lazy. The first time we did it with Banxie we did it clockwise and the full fat version. But it all went wrong fairly early on.

I am admiring the view. You can see a long way from this high, the Channel is easy to see as are the skylines of a couple of cities. Great rolling green downs, dotted with sheep (uh-oh) and lots of agriculture. If I turn around I can see the top of a fabulous natural bowl which has an interesting association with D-Day. It's a lovely day, "Lockdown" is over, for the time being, and we are sampling the great outdoors. What's not to like? That's easy, a speeding MAMIL. (I am going to assume you know what this is but just to allow me to type some venom, a MAMIL is a Middle Aged Man In Lycra - you know, a twat on a bike). He goes past, way too fast. Banxie is slightly taken aback by this, but gives a half-hearted chase, quickly stops and runs back vaguely towards us. Another MAMIL arrives but stops having seen the previous episode.

"He might run after you but he won't do anything." I reassure him.

"I want you to get your dog under control." He says, rather nastily I thought.

"That may take some time." This was probably an unhelpful comment I admit.

"You should have your dog on a lead." This was "15 all" in the unhelpful comments.

"They haven't got theirs on a lead." I said, pointing at another couple with a dog and probably getting to "30:15".

He cycled off in a huff.

When I played golf, my entire round was dictated by the first shot. If it went well, then it was okay, if it didn't then I would be on the second tee stewing about the shot on the first. This is not how to play golf, indeed it is a good metaphor for life, sometimes you just have to "let it go".

I couldn't. I was so pissed off, the MAMIL had ruined my day. The real reason was that I thought he was probably right and all us dog walkers were breaking the law. We walked on. Instead of "letting it go" my wife had to suffer a forensic analysis of the event. And do you know what? I wish, in retrospect I had just said, helpfully, making it "40:15", "Oh just piss off." Or at least commented on his MAMIL mate who clearly had no regard for anyone or anything.

But I didn't. It still bugs me today.

I am sulking as we continue the walk, Banxie is trying to cheer me up by running back and forth with his smile and luncheon meat tongue but it isn't working and, groan, someone else is coming towards us. Banxie runs to him and we chorus "Banxie here!!!" Point of pedantry, it wasn't quite a chorus because, as we know my wife can't pronounce "sy" - ha, ha!

"I don't bite." I heard. "Fuck me Banxie talks!" I thought, then realised it was this chap walking towards us, almost like the Good Samaritan.

I am going to digress again, sorry. Are you the person that the weirdo on the train sits next to? You know the one who is desperate to talk to anyone? I have been, but now I am that weirdo. Working from home wrecks any social intercourse as you spend your life cocooned in your work environment: laptop, phone, desk etc. It can be mind numbingly lonely. "Oh you work at home, lucky you." No.I.Am.Not.

So when Banxie came on the scene and I could get out and about, I found myself talking to anyone who would listen, including Banxie himself - I talk to him all the time mind you. I once walked past a garden where a man could see me talking, but couldn't actually see Banxie - "Just talking to my dog." I said as if that was completely normal - is it? And people seem happy to talk, or perhaps they are happy that the fat weirdo will be moving on soon. I think it is actually quite a nice thing, the victims might differ in opinion, but you learn some interesting stuff (e.g. river maintenance on Patch No.1), and I am also able to tell people a bit about the wildlife they can see - the owner of the three yappy dogs on $(GC)^2$ was astonished (or bored shitless) when I told him how many bird species you could see on that walk.

So I am not going to miss this opportunity, particularly as he has a T-Shirt with "Pink Floyd" written on it, my favourite band. He absolutely loves Banxie and makes a great fuss of him. To relieve my sulking a bit of catharsis is required, so I tell him the story of the MAMILs.

"Oh really, that's disappointing, should've told them to piss off."

If only. We have a too long conversation about Pink Floyd, and he tells me he worked with some of the members. I am the colour of the Downs and so it is time to move on, I can feel Banxie's and my wife's eyes boring into the back of my head.

Off we go again.

Game, set and match arrives in the shape of a signpost showing who and what, is and isn't allowed on the Downs - not a dog on a lead in any of the images at all - the MAMIL was wrong after all. I am invigorated, I am exonerated, life is good, I've won Wimbledon! We stop for lunch and it gets even better as sausage rolls are on offer - yum. Banxie gets a Kong which he licks to death and then we resume our lovely walk, Banxie walking about five times further than us, darting off into the wood and doing his gazelle impression. Further on something incredible happens. A cyclist says "thank you". No bell nor warning, that would be too much to expect, but we did get that "thank you" - amazing! Further on still we meet a couple with a dog off its lead. I just can't help myself and instead of saying "Hello, nice dog, goodbye." I do my cathartic download, the injustice has returned, and tell them the story.

"Oh really, that's disappointing, should've told them to piss off."

My chest is going to burst with triumphantness, if there is such a word. We finish the walk, I'm knackered but TH and Banxie are ready to do another circuit. Fortunately it is too late so we go home for beer - a much better idea.

The next time I visit the Downs I am alone and decide that I will again do a whole circuit clockwise. In the distance there is a lot of shooting going on and I am reminded that there's a rifle range about halfway round, but that won't be a problem because there's a path cut through the field.

We reach this field and there is a big Red Flag flying. Unfortunately the path through the field is also part of the "no-go" area. Bollocks. Guns fire. What to do? I don't really want to retrace my steps so I hatch a plan. If we walk a bit further I can cut across the next field and get back on track that way - brilliant! Ah, the road is so busy it is too dangerous. Okay, if I walk through that wood, I can get to the field etc., etc. More guns. After a bit of crashing and stumbling, Banxie and I emerge into bright sunlight on the edge of a field. I let Banxie off the lead, and unchained, he goes and bothers a covey of Red-legged Partridges (I add that to my day list, well done Banxie). I notice a Trig Point so make for that. Guns again. Now I have my bearings a quick look on my 'phone and "Bingo" I just need to go through that wood over there, and I will be back on track. I am very pleased with myself. The wood is quite sparse, this is great, almost there, oh a lovely Hazel thicket.....

Very soon I feel as if I am being shot at in some gigantic basket weaving exercise (yes I know you use reeds), I can't see anything in any direction, not even upwards, apart from Hazel trees. After five minutes I am lost. Well I know which way I should be going but can't due to the impenetrable Hazel. Big salvo. I look for Banxie, and hope against hope that he is going to turn into Charlton Heston and, "Moses-like", part the Hazel and lead me to the promised land. Banxie has other ideas, and buggers off to leave me alone. I can't see him. Two minutes pass and now I've lost him completely. The guns are silent, oh no! I've got that pissed off panicky feeling. "Banxie! Banxie!! Banxie!!!!!" I call. Nothing. I can't even hear him rustling about. Then out of nowhere he appears - phew! I get the lead on him straight away hoping he is going to start winding his way through to the "exit". Not a chance, useless mutt.

As more gunfire pierces the air I want to cry, I want my Mummy (difficult as she died in 1992). I am beginning to get a bit hypoglycaemic with all this effort but I press on. Rapid fire. About three or four hours later (five minutes) we are delivered from evil, to a barbed wire fence. Rat-a-tat-tat. I don't think I have ever been so pleased to see a barbed wire fence, until that is, I realise Banxie can't get under it. Also it is higher one side, so it will be very difficult to lift him over. I climb over, but not before I've tried to dismantle it (epic fail) and then lean over to pick up Banxie, who, understandably, is shitting himself. I am mindful of his scrotum (although it crosses my mind I could save some money here) and haul him up and over. The guns start up again. OMG I am going to faint. Luckily I have some lemonade with me, so that revives me. We resume the torture, and it is just a, not very funny, joke. Now its a fucking bramble jungle. Oh FFS! Banxie is having a right royal sniff, he is certainly on some kind of trail and lo and behold I see what looks like an animal trail that has flattened the bramble by about 0.1%. Dakkadakkadakkadakkadakka. We make our way through, getting cut and stung (nettles are there too just for fun) and finally, FINALLY, find the path - hoorayyyyyyyy!

I know where I am now. The guns are still firing away as I reach the end of the path, pleased that we managed to survive and get back on the route. Hubris turns to embarrassment as we round the corner at the end of the path and there, by the gate is a great big Red Flag. We've been through the jungle and all the time it was on the rifle range.

I am really pissed off now, it's my fault but poor old Banxie gets the grief. He won't stop pulling, probably he's desperate to get away, and I have to keep yanking him back. I am so tired and even more pissed off when I realise that there isn't a shop in the village as I had thought. We walk on with me fulminating and Banxie keeping a low profile.

In April 1989 I went to the USA for the first time. When I came back, perhaps due to the long flights (I flew from San Francisco via Boston) or the body clock effect, or the extremely hot Chinese I had eaten, I was temporarily unwell. I lay on my bed and could feel a mild pain in my bum. As time progressed it got worse and worse until, and I am not kidding, I had to bite the pillow. It was excruciating. After maybe 30 minutes the pain subsided and life went back to normal. This was my first introduction to what I believe is trapped wind. At least that's what I think it is, as there's usually the slight bonus of a fart at the end. Talking to a Physician friend of mine revealed that it could be something called "Proctalgia Fugax" - sounds awful and is - anal pain caused by intense muscle spasms in or around the canal of the anus. Nice. And it happens at night! Sounds familiar.

Since that fateful day I have had regular recurrences, probably three times a year and always, bar the first and two other occasions, at night. It is like a thunderstorm. I am awoken by a very, very slight pain and it gradually builds up into the pillow biting crescendo. In fairness, as time has progressed, either I have got used to the pain or it has lessened, but it still bloody hurts.

As I have said only 3 times has it happened in the daytime - until now. While I am moaning at Banxie, I try to ignore what I know is happening. We start to walk uphill, we are actually not far from finishing, and I can't walk properly. Banxie is now off the lead so he is having a great time whereas I am beginning to really suffer. I am not sure what to do, will walking it off effect some miracle cure, or should I lie down like normal and let it pass? I opt to walk on, but soon I can hardly move. In the end I lay down in instalments such is the pain. I inform Banxie that I need to rest and just like some tramp, I lie on the side of the path. Banxie's face says it all "WTF are you doing?" Bless him, he doesn't bear a grudge, and soon he comes over and starts pawing at me and licking my face. I think he's worried. Worried that no more treats are available. I think I pass out or sleep for a brief time, but him licking my face brings me round and I can feel the pain is subsiding. He's got his ears down, very concerned face on. He's so sweet! Five minutes later and we are on our way back to the car park, and I fart, a kind of EB moment to be honest. I wonder if I should call Charlie to tell him?

At the car park Banxie gets a drink and lots of treats for being such a tender and caring nurse, I have forgiven him for being an arse and pulling, and he has forgiven my arse, but I haven't. The only positive thing I can think is, "What a story this is going to be!"

Two more quick stories about walking around the Downs and then we are out of here. I mentioned ages ago about encountering other animals................

I had heard the gunfire as soon as I got out of the car so knew I couldn't do a loop, but for a change I decided to go anticlockwise. I arrived at the Red Flag and thought I wouldn't risk being shot at again and got ready to retrace my steps. I couldn't help but look across the fields and think that if I walked through those, I could make my own loop. A lot shorter, but at least it would be a loop, admittedly one with trespassing but hey, you've got to live, and in any case I thought we would be out of sight. As they were arable with plenty of grass at the edges, and it was past the harvest, we wouldn't be doing any harm. To be honest I am not sure if I actually did trespass, there are no signs, but I kind of assumed with a big gate we were.

Banxie was off the lead having a great time and behaving well, for him. We walked down to the bottom of the valley and on the left was a wood which was obviously not very deep as I could see a field through it. He ran off and was lost to view. Idly, I played out in my mind the scenario that would happen - I would walk past the wood, look to my left and there would be Banxie ferreting around on the edge of the wood. I was kind of right...........

I walked past the wood, looked and didn't see or hear him. I waited. I called him. Nothing. Then my eyes were attracted to a black dot in the distance. That couldn't be him, it was black for a start. Mind you at distance.........

OMFG it was him, what was he doing? Then I saw the magnet - two Roe Deer. OMFG again. He clearly wouldn't see me, and definitely wouldn't hear me, mind you neither of those things would have made him stop. I just had to wait and watch the show unfold. Initially he ran around a bit (maybe there had been a third deer that he had chased off before I got there), then he focused on one of the others. As he ran towards it I thought, it'll be fine, the deer will run off and Banxie will give up. As I watched in horror the gap between the black arrow and the deer shortened. He's going to catch it! Surely not. It seemed an age as they charged towards the edge of the field. Thank goodness, a fence

206

saved the deer, which it leapt with ease, curtailing Banxie's deer stalking performance. The other deer had gone, so left with nothing to chase the now brown arrow set his sights on me. I called him, and luncheon meat tongue hanging out he ran back and collapsed on the grass by me:

"Having fun?"

"Does a deer shit in the woods?"

"It probably just did actually."

Using a map, I measured how far he had been away from me when I saw him in the distance, just under 400m. When I measured how far he had run, it was not much less than 1km. Much as I wish he hadn't run off, I couldn't help but be mightily impressed by his speed and stamina - who's a clever boy then?

And the last bit.........we were walking back one day, not a loopy day just a "there and back" one, but I decided to mix things up a bit by walking parallel to the path through the thick grass. Banxie ran ahead, well slalomed his way ahead, when suddenly - whooosh! He accidentally flushed a bird. And this wasn't some boring partridge or pheasant but a stonking Short-eared Owl - not a common bird at all and a fine addition to my day and actually my year list. Who's a clever boy then 2.0?

I am tired now, after all that walking, but there's one more trip to tell you about. "Cliff, clear your throat mate".

WE'RE ALL GOING ON A BANXIE HOLIDAY

Here is a football result:

COVID 19 **2**   *25ᵗʰ Wedding Anniversary Holidays* **0**

Long before Banxie became part of the furniture we had booked ourselves a couple of amazing holidays to celebrate our 25ᵗʰ Wedding Anniversary. In April we were supposed to go in search of Polar Bears in Svalbard and in August and September we were meant to be travelling to first Brazil, and then Peru, spending the actual date of the anniversary at Machu Picchu. Banxie was booked in for a two week holiday with BSJ in Wales for that occasion.

A virus put paid to that. Ever resourceful we decided to try another holiday. See if you can work this one out. My wife, as you know, is from France. The capital of France is Paris, one of my favourite cities. In Paris is one of my favourite landmarks, the Eiffel Tower. We went there a few years ago (again) and one of the things she really wanted to do was visit the Eiffel Tower at night. Which we did and it was fabulous. You can't beat the Eiffel Tower, nothing comes close...........unless you're my wife.

"I've always wanted to see Blackpool." she said to me on a number of occasions. And so it was that we dreamt up a "Northern Experience" which would take in Blackpool. I mean FFS Blackpool compared with Paris, let alone Machu Picchu.

Banxie got a reprieve from BSJ's "bugger off" hospitality and joined us on this mad journey. Mind you we were all eternally grateful that we could even go anywhere. I would never have imagined in my wildest dreams that one day I would be taking a dog on holiday with me, it seemed ludicrous. But here we were barrelling up the M6 on our way to Blackpool, but via Crosby for a spot of culture.

"Another Place" by Sir Anthony Gormley consists of life-size, cast iron figures which face out to sea, spread over a 2-mile stretch of beach. The tides sweep over them and then, as they recede reveal the figures way out to sea. I didn't realise it was tidal, more gormless than Gormley, but fascinating to see the figures begin to appear as the tide ebbed.

Banxie did the decent thing and didn't crap on the beach nor piss on the figures. But he couldn't work out what they were and why there was no emotional feedback from them. So he resorted to his "default" - barking. He stood his ground and barked. And then when nothing happened he changed defaults to one of the strangest things that all dogs do, and one of the funniest. He did a "Zoomie". This is where dogs run around as if the end of the world is coming. They look mad, their heads like Tasmanian Devils as they crazily speed around a seemingly random route. I wonder what possesses them to do this, glad they do though, top notch entertainment.

Having got his fill of culture we decided to go to Blackpool. I had been there on a couple of occasions already, so briefed my wife.

"Basically a shithole with lots of fish and chip shops."

She was defiant to the end:

"Well I want to see it for myself."

Ten minutes later we had driven along the promenade and seen the Tower.

"So what do you think of Blackpool then?"

"Basically a shithole with lots of fish and chip shops."

We did go on the beach, which was actually really nice, and took a few photos for posterity (and later ridicule by our friends). Banxie didn't care, there were northern bums to be sniffed, so he was happy.

As it was a special occasion we stayed in a very nice hotel in Morecambe and got another, pleasant, shock. I had always thought hotels that were "dog friendly" did this through massively gritted teeth.

"Do you accept dogs?"

"Yes sir we do."

"Oh that's great we'd like to book the 2nd for one night please."

"Certainly, all booked sir."

End of call, scene in hotel.

"Shit we've got a bloody dog coming to stay, get that awful room 101 ready."

But it was the complete opposite of this, and not just at this hotel. In all, we stayed in seven different places and every single one made us feel very welcome and gave us decent rooms. Certainly not what we had imagined, it was really pleasing to see that we were not cast as "filthy dog botherers."

We drove all over Northern England, visiting the Lakes, Hadrian's Wall and the NE coast with its fantastic beaches before heading South, via a bit more Gormley, the wonderful "Angel of the North", for a spot of bird watching at Spurn and winding up at York on the last day, just so I could achieve an ambition and spend some time with a different sort of "Mallard" - I'll admit, I got emotional seeing that great leviathan of steam from a completely different age - a beauty.

And throughout our absolutely marvellous time Banxie was a star. Well, most of the time.......

I lived in the Lake District when I was a student back in 1980. I worked at Windscale, or Sellafield as it was known then - it regularly changes its name to try and fool the public as something else dodgy happens there - nuclear fires, missing plutonium etc. While I was there, (126 days, not that I was counting) I was without a car so really didn't get to see the Lakes much at all. I had always had a bit of a thing about climbing Scafell Pike (the highest mountain in England), I even bought a "Wainwright" book, but time passed and now some 40 years later I thought the opportunity had gone, largely due to it being so far away but probably more because of being the FH and unfit.

But I put it on our itinerary. For months before I imagined walking up there. I talked to Banxie all the time about what it would be like and wondered whether I would make it. I did a fair bit of research

211

on this, looking at routes and looking at whether dogs could climb it. The results weren't encouraging. Wainwright said the route we would take was something like "a boring slog" and other information suggested that if your dog is not used to fell walking then Scafell Pike is very definitely NOT the place to start, with a particular emphasis on the last bit of the ascent through the boulder field. It said how "dogs have been Medivaced off Scafell Pike", and that "serious injuries can result" - sounded great! We decided we would have a "look see" and if Banxie was looking knackered or struggling, we would stop. The other caveat was that he would probably need to be on a lead for most of it. As the FH and unfit, TH agreed, bless her, to take full responsibility for his welfare.

The great day came, it had been pissing down all day before, and we set off into the grey mist. The first bit was not too bad at all, I thought "this is going to be a piece of piss." We met a guy coming down quite early on, and of course, running my "Weirdo On The Train Situation" app (WottsApp, I thank you), I had to talk to him. Apparently the Lingmell Gill, a river, was in spate after the rain and you couldn't cross it without getting very wet. My initial thought was "at least I can say I tried.". We decided to carry on and reaching Lingmell Gill dicked around for 20 minutes before my wife basically said "Fuck it" picked Banxie up and marched across - done!

The weather was awful, cold and misty but we carried on. Seeing lots of other dogs was heartening and naturally I had to WottsApp the owners and ask about conditions - all fine thankfully. I said I wouldn't try to keep up with my wife and Banxie so I would meet them at the summit if I made it. The bastards then buggered off!

WottsApp went into overdrive as I climbed higher and felt more and more knackered. Everyone I passed I asked "How far is it?" - it always seemed to be about 1.5 hours. One guy I met I asked a different question:

"Please tell me this is the worst bit."

"Sorry it's not, it gets worse and steeper and it's about an hour and a half from here." said Job's comforter.

I was broken. But occasionally I could see Banxie jumping about in the distance so that spurred me on. As I looked underfoot I was expecting to catch them up, it was very rough and I was sure bouncy Banxie was going to come a cropper sooner or later - but nope. After what seemed liked weeks, I got to a part of the climb and the sun actually shone briefly revealing the cairn at the summit - my God I am going to make it - I had a tear in my eye.

Not long after I reached the summit to be greeted by two soaking wet and very cold life forms, one saying and one intimating "What kept you? We've been here 25 minutes". I didn't feel in the least bit bad about that. Banxie was delighted to see me and he was fit as a fiddle, no injuries, nothing. We all climbed up the little man made cairn, which is now the actual summit, got blown to bits, took the obligatory photo and then went to shelter from the wind. I had been there perhaps five minutes.

"Okay let's go then."

"WTF?!"

And we were off, no rest for FH, but an egg mayonnaise sandwich wasn't so shabby.

The descent was a piece of piss compared to the ascent (apart from aching quads) and I was on a high. Mainly because I was delighted to have achieved a long held ambition, but also because Banxie had done it easily without any injury and had behaved himself impeccably. That was until we were about half way down.

As I rounded a corner, there was my wife frantically trying to move Banxie, who was firmly clamped on a walker's shin, pumping for England.

"Don't worry I've got one of these at home." he said.

I assumed he meant a dog, rather than some bizarre sex toy. We declamped Banxie and moved on and back to the hotel for tea and medals - "who's a clever boy then, FH?" said Banxie. It took me four days to recover from that walk, I swear that Banxie was up for it again as soon as we had had tea and the medal ceremony - he is so fit!

Twice more he disgraced himself. It is easy to know when it is happening, the world goes silent. In one hotel I caught him eating the covers on the arms of the sofa. My wife, ever resourceful, sewed them back up, and with strategically placed cushions nobody would have known. And later still he decided he would bonk then rip a pillow case up. This was slightly more difficult to hide, but we did our best.

"Well you pay extra for the dog, so they must expect some damage."

I hope we were right. Nobody ever said anything so either they did expect damage or my wife will be appearing on "The Repair Shop" soon.

So that was Banxie's first holiday, and it was brilliant! Lovely places, lovely scenery and lots of walking. The only problem with the North seemed to be the number of sheep. They were everywhere! Fortunately we got expert at sheep spotting so were able to get Banxie on the lead before any havoc ensued.

Let's not forget the people. I decided that the friendliest bunch of people in the world are "walkers". Everyone one of them was pleasant, was fine with Banxie if he jumped up (he was getting much better at not doing this) and happy to share information - I really appreciated that there were so many kind human beings in the world for a change. But then we were "oop Nurth" - and Northerners are far more friendly than Southerners (and I am one) - fact.

We returned home and as a reward for being such a good dog, Banxie got a visit to the Vet, "Who's a castrated boy then?"

DOGILOGUE

One morning when I was writing this Banxie seemed to be paying an awful lot of attention as he sat on the floor by my desk. He leapt up and started pawing at me, growling too - this was odd, it was as if he wanted to tell me something....and once again thanks to a Dogger using Doggle Translate, Banxie has this to say......

Talk about bad press! If you've just read this then let me tell you that it's a completely biased account by FH. I really am not that bad at all, the trouble is he, and to some extent the others, haven't worked it out yet.

I'll give them 9/10 for the accommodation and food. (I might write that up on Sniff Advisor). The reason I docked them one point is because of that second crate - I mean come on. I didn't want to stay in that awful thing. And my plan worked, barking that was irritating enough to get the idiots to let me have the bed - ha, the luxury!

When it comes to training, well FH is FH - fucking hopeless! That's unkind, he does his best but he just isn't firm enough. He's like Sergeant Wilson in Dad's Army "Er, if you could just come over here Banxie, that'd be awfully nice of you." I need "Here, now!" TH is not bad but their son is best. He's brutal, he scares the shit out of me, no voice, just signs - but at least I know where I am. Talking of scaring the shit out of me, the daughter, a bloody bastard Vet, good at picking me up I will admit, I can get "really close to her" (wink, wink) but more interested in my arsehole than anything else. I fear it every time she shows up.

Training has been a bit sketchy, but at least with my humans it is vastly better than that omnishambles of "Recall". FFS I hated that! Look, I can do recall, I know what it is, it's just that it's not that important to me. I want to run and sniff not constantly come back to see you - I get to see you all the time, too much methinks. And treats - meh. Get some new ones if you really want me to come back, I'm sick of that crap you currently have. But keep the rabbit's ears, I like them. Oh and by the way, my name is "Banxie" isn't it? What's with this pretentious "Banquo" shit and "Banks"? "Banxie". End of.

On a plus point - walking - well I do get great exercise and go to some lovely places. But please can you make sure you check out the routes before we go? I am sick of getting shot at, walking off-piste and getting lost in jungles and I am more than happy not to visit the seaside - it sucks. Oh and bird watching? My God that is so boring, that's why I run off and disappear, just to get you moving again! Can you try to leave your binoculars at home for once? And yes I do deliberately wander left and right, in front and behind just to wind you up!

Going to a walk in the car. Frankly I don't think I can give you any more hints about the car. I hate it. But.....I will put up with it for a short while. You see I did feel very, very sick to start with, but have managed to control that. I know I look miserable as sin and don't eat treats in the car, but that is part of my act. One thing that would help is if you actually cleaned the bloody thing. You make me get in it and it is downright filthy, disgusting. I might be a dog, but I have principles you know. And that hose thing you use. FFS put some warm water in it will you? It's bloody freezing!

Sorry about the lawn, can't help it, like a drug, see a bit of green and just have to dig it up. But I promise I will try to improve on that. Also, you can leave me for a few hours here and there, I can look after myself you know.

217

Last, but not least - again I've tried to hint but, can I have a new food bowl please, my current one looks like someone ran through it with an AK47!

THE END

The mangled body of what was once a lively, fun loving dog lies in the gutter of the road:

"I'm so sorry, he's been run over. He's dead, the car didn't even stop."

"Where did it happen?"

"On the main road up there, he just ran across the road and the car hit him."

"Would you bury him at midnight on the lawn?"

"Yes, okay I can do that"

"I'd like you to do it at about that time, I'll be away with work."

"I'll see it's done."

The doors show the scratch marks and there's the lead hanging up on the wall - reminders of times gone by, a truly bittersweet moment......

And it did happen, but not in 2020, this was 16th May 1943, and the dog was Wing Commander Guy Gibson's dog. I can't type his name as it is not politically correct to do so, shame, I hate rewriting history, but let's just say it is, in current times, an unpleasant synonym of "black".

Shortly before he was due to lead the Dambuster's raid his dog was killed by a car, which really didn't stop - how shabby was that? I wonder how Gibson felt? His mind must've been like a box of frogs that day - his dog killed and about to embark on one of the most dangerous bombing raids ever. But perhaps the concentration required got him through the grief?

I am in the inner sanctum, probably reading the Beano, I've fast forwarded almost 27 years, it's 30th March 1970. My fat cousin, of Penny the Corgi fame, has had a baby, it's the first Grandchild for my parents' siblings. My mind drifts to my paternal Grandmother who died a few years before, I have no idea why she crosses my mind, I hardly knew her. All too quickly the worst connection of neurons in my life occurs. I think how my father must have been upset when his mother died, and then I realise my own mortality. I shiver. I can't process it, I can't believe it. It can't be true? But it is. I am going to cark it myself one day. And right there starts, to date, over 50 years of torment. I look back and think, if this happened today I would receive counselling, it may even be diagnosed as a "nervous breakdown" - at almost 11 years of age?

It has sometimes been very difficult to deal with, particularly when I was young. That's ironic really, I'd have thought I would get worse as time progressed. It's an unwelcome visitor, an infrequent constant that, like my painful arse problem, only attacks me at night, ha, ha perhaps they are related? I can wake up at night, think of death and shudder, it's terrifying, but thankfully the feeling disappears quite quickly.

Nobody gave me any help at home. My mother was constantly in and out of mental homes so I suspect they didn't really want to acknowledge another nutjob in the household. I did talk to my older sister about it, her advice was "It happens to everyone, there's nothing you can do about it, so just get on with life." Not bad, and it works for a while, but always it comes back to haunt me. Such awful morbid thoughts about people, things, situations, it ruins me sometimes. I remember my parents were taking me and a friend to the (excellent) Bovington Tank Museum back in the summer of 1970. As I got in the back of the car I thought "I am going to die one day" and that was it - day ruined. Mind in "morbid thought" mode all day. My niece, of Pilot fame, says it's my subconscious wanting to protect - I like that idea, but somehow I would've thought my overactive brain would play out nice thoughts to inspire protection, not the horrid stuff I have showing in the cinema of my mind.

I am not sure what I am worried about? Is it that I am worried about how I will die or is it more arrogant, "How on earth will the world survive without me?!" Daft I know.

I'm at the Vet, it is now another 38 years later still. In my arms is "Zizi" our cat of 18 years. An absolute trooper, the nicest cat I ever knew. He's not in good shape, off his food, and appears as if he is walking on "Smarties Tubes", he's in agony I think.

My wife has whisked the kids off to town "in case".

I am crying, and Zizi pisses himself. The Vet, she's Italian, brings a towel.

"Is that for me or the cat?". I try some black humour but the elephant in the room doesn't disappear.

221

"Soa, youa thinka eeta time fora thea enda orva hees liefa"

I nod solemnly.

She does the business, and I stay with him watching him drift away.

It is fucking horrible. I go home. My wife arrives and I open the door.

"I'm afraid he didn't make it." I announce.

It is fucking horrible again. My daughter dissolves, my wife is upset and my son goes upstairs. I find him a bit later crying his eyes out, I never even knew he was that fond of the cat.

I vow that I will never, ever take an animal to a Vet to be "euthanised" again.

And now we have Banxie. If you use that formula that one human year is equivalent to seven dog years (yes I know it is rubbish but bear with) then Banxie and I are going to reach 70 around the same time give or take.

We will both be in our dotage, and I am hoping that I am still out there walking and he is still walking with me - albeit both of us somewhat slower, and no doubt fatter in my case. We will be looking out for each other. But as Oscar Wilde said, while he lay in a fleapit of a hotel in Paris looking at his surroundings:

"My wallpaper and I are fighting a duel to the death. One or the other of us has to go."

And the truth is, unless there is some truly horrid coincidence, then one of us has to go first. If it is me, then Banxie might be upset, but I am sure a rabbit ear and the sniff of a new arse will sort him out, I can't see him doing a "Greyfriars Bobby" for me. But if it is the other way round, well it doesn't bear thinking about, I am welling up just writing this. I know I would have to go to the Vet with him, it would be an act of cowardice not to. Maybe, the Vet could visit us though? Whatever, Banxie will get wind of what is happening; how could I look into those eyes, into his soul for that last time, and see him looking back at me?

This scenario had crossed my mind even before we decided to get a dog - the ultimate what if? It's horrid, but, it is something you have to consider, or perhaps you're happy to sweep it under the carpet, with all the other dog hairs and treats and get on with it? And I don't blame you, I wish I could. Most of the time I can too, but there's a nasty spirit that sits on my shoulder and throws darts at my face from time to time - an absolute bastard it is.

While I cannot label it as a "trial run", I got a taster of life without him when I snuck off to the Scilly Isles for a spot of bird watching with my friend from "Steps". This was the first time I had ever been away from Banxie, and if I am honest, I thought it would be a welcome relief. I certainly slept well, that's for sure, although that may have been due more to beer than a lack of Fischer and Kasparov disturbing my slumber.

223

We walked miles on Scilly and inevitably met lots of other walkers, many with dogs. My WottsApp ran riot. I simply had to stop and talk to the owners, always adding "I am sure your dog can smell my dog." It was like a "proud parent moment", telling them about Banxie, but really I think I was subconsciously "keeping in touch" and wondering what he was up to - chewing something probably. I really did miss him, far more than I thought. I felt guilty leaving him and even more so when I walked miles without him. But of course he didn't care and besides he was well looked after.

When I got back, I called my wife to say I was outside. This was tactics, in case of a massive "Happy Wee". Banxie came out, saw me and went nuts. He made this incredible noise, a sort of whimpering but not too plaintive, I think he was pleased to see me - it was mutual. He didn't wee thank goodness. Then he did a Zoomie, just to remind me what a card-carrying nutjob he is - I wouldn't want him to be any other way.

I am about to go downstairs. Banxie will be in his bed and will stay there because, for some odd reason, he always seems to think he is in trouble when he is left alone. I suspect, dare I mention it, that this is our fault - we are with him so much he probably thinks not being with us is a punishment. But I know that when I get a chew out and dip it in peanut butter all will be right in his world. And it is, he sits there with the chew sticking out the side of his mouth, big blob of peanut butter on the tip, and for me he is reminiscent of Noel Coward in a smoking jacket "How do I look? Cool?"

I will have some breakfast (probably give him some, that's wrong too) and then we will have the "Lead-and-Harness-Putting-On-Ceremony" and we will go out for a walk - it will be $(GC)^2$ today; who will we meet and what will we see? - that's for me, Banxie is more "What smells will I discover today, and will FH keep calling me back for treats?"

I am pleased that Banxie is not perfect, he really is Dennis The Menace, but he's also a cool dude too, a rebel with paws (geddit?). And he is my Muse, okay I know they were female. Sometimes Thalia, the Muse of Comedy, sometimes Melpomene, the Muse of Tragedy, and often, on the lead, the little bastard is Terpsichore, the Muse of Dance.

But I can forgive him all his failings, because his plus points, and the benefit of having him with me, far outweighs the negatives. He simply wouldn't be the dog that I know and love if he was perfect. He's been an absolute shining star in my life, helped me lose weight and given me a purpose (code for kick up the arse) in my rather sedentary life; he's got me out of bed in the morning, not always for good reasons, it has to be said, thinking back to piles of poo. He listens to my inane ramblings, puts up with incessant stops to look at birds and to bore people shitless with my WottsApp yet he never judges me - or at least I don't think he does.

There's only one Banxie, and Banxie you're my hero!

225

"Let's go for a walk shall we?"

You know the rest.

ACKNOWLEDGEMENTS

Firstly, thank you to all those walkers and dog owners that Banxie and I have met, (and Banxie has jumped up on, sorry), whose names I do not know. 99.99% of you were very accommodating and we thank you for that. And thank you to the two cyclists, out of hundreds, who actually stopped for us once - miracles can happen. To Phil and Shelley the owners of Winston and Maisie who created Banxie! Also to Courtney Goodchild of Olympia Publishers. Without her request for the rest of the manuscript (after I'd sent a sample), which I hadn't yet written, I'd never have finished it - so even though they didn't give me a publishing deal at least they did help!

Lots of Twitterati and elsewhere have helped, can't name everyone but thanks to Nicola Neyhaul, Gillian Membury, Nazim, Gary Wilkinson. I'd particularly like to thank MSA Birder, Richard Farrar, The SPN Archive, and Cumpy for their excellent p-woof reading, and Chris Roseveare FRCP for excellent suggestions right from the start.

Thanks also to my future son-in-law for owning BSJ, and giving us a taster of what owning a dog would be like - where it all started really.

Most importantly, thanks to my lovely French wife, my daughter "the resident Vet" and my son, the journalistic "voice of reason" for their input in naming Banxie and for putting up with me all these years!

Oh, I nearly forgot, tsk, tsk, of course I need to say a special "thank you" to my muse Banxie, without whom none of this would have happened. Imagine how peaceful that would have been, and how dull.

227

AND JUST ONE LAST THING

I wonder if any of you have pondered on the slightly curious spelling of Banxie. Those birdwatchers amongst you, (none then) might have thought I spelt it like that because it is close to "Bonxie", the Gaelic word for the Great Skua. Here comes the truth. Banxie is actually spelt "Banksy". Like the artist. We didn't name him after the artist, we just thought it was a good name.

Sadly it was too good a name to use because the real Banksy's "management", Pest Control as they are called, said they might sue me if I used that spelling. "English multi-millionaire street artist, political activist, and film director sues English nobody" - I can see the headlines now. I was quite bullish and was reminded of Oscar Wilde (well Monty Python really) and "there's only one thing in the world worse than being talked about, and that's not being talked about." Imagine the publicity, the sales, the legal costs!

I sought help on Twitter, and I'm extremely grateful to Aaron Wood, an IP Lawyer who gave me some free advice, which was "don't". Unlike Banxie, I do know what "don't" means, so I didn't. Hence Banksy was reborn as Banxie, but only temporarily of course.

D O'Gowner   December 2020

Tier 2

Printed in Great Britain
by Amazon

67425524R00132